Informed Answers

to

Gay Rights Questions

Roger Magnuson

MULTNOMAH

Sisters, Oregon

INFORMED ANSWERS TO GAY RIGHTS QUESTIONS

published by Multnomah Books
a part of the Questar publishing family

© 1994 by Roger J. Magnuson

International Standard Book Number: 0-88070-7

Cover designed by Multnomah Graphics

Printed in the United States of America

Unless noted otherwise, Scripture quotations are from The King James
Version

For information:
QUESTAR PUBLISHERS, INC.
POST OFFICE BOX 1720
SISTERS, OREGON 97759

94 95 96 97 98 99 00 01 02 — 10 9 8 7 6 5 4 3 2 1

"The process of living
seems to consist in coming to realize truths
so ancient and simple that,
if stated,
they sound like barren platitudes."
—C. S. Lewis

CONTENTS

13   **INTRODUCTION: Why This Book Is Important**

27   **1. THE AGENDA: What Homosexuals Really Want**

27.   a. "All we want is tolerance, not approval of our lifestyle. We want to be allowed to be in the mainstream of American life and not be kept on the margins of society."

29   b. "This is all about having the same rights other people do. We're not asking for special preferences."

34   c. "We have no secret agenda. We simply want to be treated like other people."

41   d. "Don't blame us for the demands of some fringe activists or extremists. All we want is what you already have."

45   **2. THE APPROACH: Take the Offensive, and Stay Away from Behavior**

45   a. "We should show sensitivity to gay men and lesbians in their quest for dignity and basic civil rights."

47   b. "We need to do something to stop gay bashing!"

48   c. "But for your homophobia, you would see our side, too. You seem to be fascinated by sex and sleaze and have used all kinds of false and distorted information. I am disappointed that you manifest such homophobia, hate mongering, and bigotry."

51   d. "No one chooses to be a homosexual or can be 'recruited' into this lifestyle. Do you think anyone would choose to suffer like we do?"

53   e. "Call us by our name. We are gay people."

55   f. "We have to make it unlawful for people to use hate speech against minorities. The paradox is this: We have no free speech right ourselves unless hate speech is banned."

56   g. "You are Nazis at heart. They persecuted homosexuals, too."

59   **3. THE AUTHENTICATION: Why It Is Important for Homosexuals to Misrepresent Who and How Many They Are (and Were)**

59   a. "We represent ten percent, perhaps fifteen percent, of the population. How can you deny us our rights?"

63   b. "You may not appreciate this, but gay people have a long and illustrious history. Alexander the Great, Jonathan and David, Plato, Michelangelo, and a host of others have made major contributions to society."

67   c. "There are far more of us than you realize. We are all around you. We are your fathers, mothers, brothers and sisters, sons and daughters."

68   d. "We have the support of most of the religious leadership in our campaign."

74   e. "Psychologists now recognize that we are not 'sick' or 'mentally ill.' Compelled by scientific evidence, they took homosexuality off a list of mental disorders in the early 70s."

77   f. "We are as normal as 'straight' people."

81   **4. THE "ALL GOD'S CHILDREN" CLAIM: Why Homosexuals Claim That Nature Makes Them Do It (Sometimes), Even Though the Assertion Is Demonstrably False**

81   a. "No one seriously believes homosexuality is somehow an acquired behavior."

83   b. "Biology now has confirmed that being gay is genetically determined. It is no longer open to serious question."

85   c. "Some people are right-handed and some people are left-handed. Some are gay and some are straight. No one chooses his or her sexual orientation. No one can change it."

88   d. "It's terribly unfair to permit discrimination against someone who can't help the way he or she is."

91   **5. THE ARGUMENT: How Doing Sexually Deviant Acts Can Make a Minority Worthy of Civil Rights Protection**

91   a. "We're not asking for anything special. We only want what heterosexual couples have."

94   b. "We are a legitimate minority, just like those who have won similar protections before us."

100   c. "We have been subject to a pernicious pattern of discrimination. We have been denied basic rights and privileges. We are an underclass."

104   d. "All the diverse ways people live together should be treated equally by the law. How would you like to be unemployed and homeless simply because others don't approve of your lifestyle?"

104   e. "Don't confuse the issue with scare stories about churches. Free expression is protected by the Constitution. Churches are not affected by gay rights laws."

106   f. "Who is hurt by giving us our rights?"

117   **6. THE AMORAL ORTHODOXY: How Homosexuals Promote The View That Sex Has No Moral Boundaries**

117   a. "There is nothing wrong with sex. Sex is pleasurable and harmless, unless it is done in a way that is exploitative or coercive."

119   b. "We must appreciate our differences, and stop looking down on people who do things differently. Christians should recognize that there is nothing inherently better or worse about homosexuality or heterosexuality."

119   c. "Using the cultural prejudices of the Bible to endorse homophobia is un-Christian. New Testament condemnations of homosexuality reflect cultural prejudice and don't address loving, committed homosexual relationships."

121   d. "The Bible does not condemn committed, loving relationships between people of the same sex."

125   e. "God loves gay people, too."

125   f. "Jesus never condemned homosexuality."

125   g. "The Church has always taught that sex is sinful."

126   h. "Doesn't the Bible say that we should judge not lest we be judged?"

126   i. "The Old Testament references used against gay sex are taken out of context and usually were part of ceremonial laws that, if we obeyed them, would have us all refusing to wear fabrics and not shaving our beards."

127   j. "The Bible condemns only homosexual behavior that is a part of pagan religious exercises."

127   k. "The incident of Sodom shows how people misunderstand what the Bible says about sexual relationships."

129   l. "True Christianity is compassionate. It is summed up in love. It doesn't seek to change people; it accepts them."

133   7. THE AVOIDANCE FACTOR: What Homosexuals Must Cover Up about Typical Same-Sex Lifestyles

133   a. "Don't use homophobic stereotypes. Judge us individually. You can't generalize about any group."

135   b. "Gay people are not different in their behavior from other people."

143   c. "Gay people have no more physical or psychological problems than anyone else."

148   d. "Gay people, in fact, are less violent and less likely to commit child abuse."

149   8. THE AIDS SPIN

149   a. "Homophobic people have spread myths about AIDS to bias people against gays."

151   b. "AIDS is not a gay disease. It is everyone's disease."

153   c. "The bias of the government is shown by its refusal to deal with AIDS and to commit the necessary resources to deal with it."

155   d. "Until the government starts spending enough money to find a cure, the best we can do is AIDS education efforts in our schools, with a special emphasis on condom use."

157   9. THE "PRIVACY" APPEAL: Are Sexual Behaviors Entitled To Confidentiality?

157   a. "What people do in their own bedrooms is nobody's business but theirs."

161   b. "People have a constitutional right to do whatever they want to if it's consensual and doesn't affect some third party."

164   c. "We want nothing more than to be left alone."

165   10. AIN'T NOBODY IN HERE BUT US CHICKENS: How Homosexuals Seek to Put the Best Foot Forward, Even While Carrying Water for Child Molesters and Others

165   a. "You distort homosexual behaviors by stereotypes. We are monogamous, too."

167   b. "The real child molesters are heterosexuals."

170   c. "We're not asking for special protection for illegal activity of any kind."

173   CONCLUSION: Informed Answers to Gay Rights Questions

175   ENDNOTES

INTRODUCTION:
Why This Book Is Important

Militant homosexuals are on the march. Their goal is total social acceptance and legal sanction of their behavior and lifestyle, and they have made inroads seemingly everywhere. State and local governments across the country have been inundated with proposed pro-homosexual legislation. Even the president of the United States has rallied to the cause of homosexuals. Someday, the homosexual parade may reach your own doorstep.

This is why you and other concerned Americans need to read a book about this abnormality called homosexuality, becoming educated on issues that are both distasteful and unrelated to us personally—issues that you may find repulsive. It isn't enough to know that sodomy is immoral. The political proposals advanced by an increasingly aggressive group of homosexual activists, who demand full social acceptance of sexual deviance, will continue to drastically alter the fabric of American culture, if left unchecked. Critical public policy issues can only be properly addressed and challenged by educated, informed people.

It's time for serious discussion and reasoned analysis of the issue of homosexuality and the specific demands made by homosexual activists. Unfortunately, gay rights proposals have often received neither. There has been a curious inversion of what one would expect—a high level of public policy interest, but a low level of public policy debate. To be effective citizens, we need to understand the issues of the debate and the importance of it. And the debate is indeed extremely important, as we shall see.

First, let's look at some strategies of gay rights proponents. **The tactics of gay rights activists are designed to avoid at all costs serious analysis of their agenda, and can be successfully resisted only by careful and reasoned argument.**

Those who have studied homosexual initiatives have observed a fourfold tactical plan:

1. Avoid, whenever possible, serious public debate over gay rights measures. Gay rights measures are often timed to surprise possible opponents. They are frequently introduced toward the end of a legislative session, and in haste. In states with no referendum procedure, they are usually proposed in off years so legislators who vote for them need not fear a personal referendum that could lead to removal from office. Often, homosexuals seek to persuade governors or mayors to issue executive orders barring "discrimination" on the basis of "sexual orientation," effectively insulating the issue from the political process or from careful consideration by elected representatives. More recently, homosexuals have tried to repeal popular referendum provisions in city charters before seeking to pass gay rights laws, to avoid full-scale debate and democratic resolution of the issue.

These tactics are understandable, as a political matter, but hardly ideal if one desires sensible analysis and reasoned debate.

2. If public debate is imminent, seek to intimidate opposing voices into silence. The militant homosexual movement has not distinguished itself for tolerance to opposing views, or even for good manners and common courtesy. The examples are plentiful:

• Adam Walinsky, a New York City public official and former adviser to Senator Robert Kennedy, opposes a gay rights measure in his city. His house is set on fire.

• A major eastern college threatens Christian groups with loss of campus accreditation and expulsion for inviting a speaker to the campus to discuss the public policy ramifications of gay rights measures.

• Gay rights groups seek to impeach a student body president at the University of Minnesota for expressing an opinion supporting the U.S. Army position on homosexuality, a position frequently ratified by federal courts.

• A symposium is held in Southern California. Among the guests are a respected congressman and the chairman of the United States Civil Rights Commission. Homosexual activists threaten the hotel that has agreed to host the event. The hotel breaches its agreement and cancels the reservations. Another hotel is booked. Homosexuals visit the hotel in the early morning hours and set off stink bombs. The leader of the homosexuals publishes in the local newspaper a thinly veiled personal threat to the chairman of the Civil Rights Commission, suggesting that he bear in mind before coming to speak that the homosexuals know where he lives. They then later seek to invade the meeting and "shut it down."

• Prominent psychiatrists are shouted down as Nazis. A leading psychotherapist privately tells organizers of a symposium critical of gay rights that he agrees entirely with their position as a matter of public policy but is afraid to appear on a public panel.

• In Minneapolis, a member of the city council introduces a measure to control "cruising" for boy prostitutes in a downtown park. The park, long a haven for juvenile prostitution, has frequently had cars circling it nearly bumper to bumper at 2:00 in the morning. The council member, a woman, has long supported gay rights measures. But a group of "Friends Against Gay Suppression" (FAGS) storm her house, beat on the door with traffic pylons and, when her husband comes out to plead with them to disperse, throw him to the ground.

• Thomas Sowell relates in his book, *Inside American Education,*[1] the story of Samuel Burke, a particularly compelling example of the intimidating, implacable practices of homosexuals on modern campuses.

> At Harvard, a freshman named Samuel Burke inadvertently got into trouble in December 1985, while merely trying to help some strangers find a table on which to eat lunch in a crowded dining room. Spotting an empty table, he removed a sign that read: "Reserved HRGLSA," and invited them to sit there. It turned out that those initials stood for the Harvard Radcliffe Gay and Lesbian Students Association—which made this an ideological offense against one of the "in" groups. Sam Burke was taken to the freshman dean's office. According to the *Harvard Salient,* a student publication:
>
> "Sam offered to apologize to the GLSA for his thoughtless act. But according to friends, he was nonetheless pushed to the brink of tears by the official inquisitors who questioned his motives at every turn and threatened him with severe punishment."
>
> Heavy pressure on this young man, at an institution where deliberate disruption and even violence have repeatedly gone unpunished, was all the more remarkable because the freshman dean's office knew that Samuel Burke was already burdened with personal problems. A high school

football star, he had just been told by a physician that he could not play football in college. Moreover, his father had recently been killed in an automobile accident. But no humane considerations tempered the zeal of those determined to do the politically correct thing. Sam Burke was hit with disciplinary probation just before the Christmas holidays.

He did not return from the holidays. He committed suicide.[2]

The intolerance is almost entirely one way. Homosexual speakers are not generally shouted down, disinvited, or threatened. But those who do not share their views often remain silent for fear of loss of academic status, personal intimidation, or physical safety. Many voices that need to be heard are not.

3. If debate occurs, use ad hominem *arguments.* The homosexual activists like to characterize themselves as spokesmen for a rational, compassionate, and progressive enlightenment and their opponents as spokesmen for a superstitious, insensitive, regressive ignorance.

But when the debate is on, homosexual activists frequently resort to name-calling, while their opponents recite facts. Adam Walinsky may have admired Senator Kennedy on civil rights, but he is now a "bigot." Dr. Socarides may be a civil libertarian, but if he disagrees with homosexuals on whether their behavior is an illness, he is a bigot, too. Any resistance to the homosexual agenda is a product of "homophobia" or "erotophobia." Sophisticated name-calling may be good strategy in the modern battle of the sound bite, but it does little to advance public understanding of what is at stake.

4. If the debate goes beyond ad hominem *labeling, avoid at all costs discussion of homosexual behavior.* Homosexual strategy is simple: Keep the discussion as abstract as possible—civil rights, discrimination, minority status. Avoid being drawn into discussion of homosexual behavior. If someone brings up embarrassing facts about the homosexual lifestyle, accuse the person of being obsessed with sex and the merely physical dimension of human relationships.

The privileges sought for practitioners of homosexual behavior require a serious look at homosexual behavior. What *do* they do? What impact does what they do have on society? On themselves? But the conscious avoidance of such difficult (and unflattering) issues by proponents of gay rights invite policy makers to buy a pig in a poke—to extend social legitimacy to a lifestyle they only dimly understand.

Second, **most people underestimate the serious implications of homosexuality.** Thorough analysis of this issue is required. Widespread acceptance of homosexuality is peculiarly destructive to society. In the Old Testament, God repeatedly links sodomy and infanticide as two "abominations" for which he judges a nation. They are the two issues which cause a people to be vomited out of their land. Jewish social commentator Dennis Prager, in his article, "Homosexuality, the Bible, and Us,"[3] concludes:

> And the bedrock of this civilization, and of Jewish life, of course, has been the centrality and purity of family life. But the family is not a natural unit so much as it is a *value* that must be cultivated and protected. The Greeks assaulted the family in the name of beauty and Eros. The Marxists assaulted the family in the name of progress. And, today, gay liberation assaults it in the name of compassion and equality. I understand why gays would do this. Life has

been miserable for many of them. What I have not understood is why Jews and Christians would join the assault.

I do now. They do not know what is at stake. At stake is our civilization.[4]

Third, **the surprising successes of homosexuals in overcoming obstacles, without being subjected to any kind of clear field analysis, makes study of the issue imperative.** The difference in intensity between the best and the worst is nowhere confirmed more graphically than in the growing power of homosexual rights organizations in America. Their intensity and surprising successes cause many to wonder whether Yeats's pessimism is justified: "Things fall apart, the center cannot hold."

The obstacles these groups have faced, and to some degree surmounted, are formidable:

• Laws in many states making consensual sodomy criminal.

• The natural revulsion normal people feel in the face of sexual perversion—a reaction homosexuals refer to as "homophobia."

• The documented history of wild promiscuity suggesting that the average male homosexual has had over five hundred different partners.

• Enormous public health costs caused directly and indirectly by homosexual conduct (homosexuals, though perhaps fewer than five percent of the population, carry a majority of the nation's syphilis).

• A major role in the AIDS epidemic, which according to the *Wall Street Journal* will cost the economy over sixty billion dollars in the next year.

• A historic timidity about revealing perverse sexual practices to family and friends, what homosexuals call "coming out."

Notwithstanding these obstacles, homosexuals have made surprising progress. The modern university campus is a good example of homosexual influences.

• Thomas Sowell points out in his book that the playing field is not level.[5] He states:

> Being non-judgmental in one direction is part of the double standards surrounding the "politically correct" social agenda on many campuses. For example, homosexuals are free to publicly proclaim the merits of their lifestyle, as they see it, but anyone who publicly proclaims the demerits of that lifestyle, as he sees it, is subject to serious punishment. At Yale University, for example, "Gay and Lesbian Awareness Days" have been an annual event celebrating homosexuality. A sophomore with different views put up posters parodying the homosexuals' posters. For this alone, he was suspended for two years. The dean of Yale's own law school called the decision "outrageous."[6] In the face of this and other outcries, Yale reduced the punishment to probation—with a warning that anything like this again would mean expulsion.

• A Wesleyan University student reported a similar situation there:

> It is nearly impossible to enter the campus center without being inundated by propaganda about gay men, lesbian women, and bisexuals.[7]

"Re-education" is a common punishment for those judged guilty of such ideological crimes as "homophobia." At the University of Vermont, a fraternity which rescinded an invitation to a pledge when they learned that he was homosexual, had among its punishments attendance at workshops and lectures against "homophobia."[8] Homosexuals are only one of a number of special groups about whom students are no longer free to have their own opinions, nor are free to choose not to associate, even though such groups remain free to be as separatist and exclusive as they wish.

• Lesbians at Mount Holyoke scribble "Lesbians Make Great Lovers," and "Try It You'll Like It" on campus sidewalks. Harvard homosexual groups staple pictures of people engaged in sodomy on kiosks. Bathrooms have to be periodically steel-plated at the University of Florida, Dartmouth, and Georgetown from the zealous use of "glory holes" in restrooms to facilitate anonymous sexual encounters. But any contrary opinion, one consistent with millennia of moral teaching and traditional moral values, will be mocked—or punished—into silence.

Fourth, **without a clear understanding of the issue, those who oppose gay rights sometimes become unduly pessimistic.** Faced with these developments, the average citizen sometimes feels like a pedestrian standing between the tracks, shouting "halt" to a roaring locomotive. The opposition attempts to create a sense of historical inevitability about these social changes. Some politicians are inordinately influenced by a small but determined minority of homosexual militants. And the media dish out megadoses of propaganda that define the issues in a way most favorable to the homosexual agenda. A great iron triangle of a special-interest group (the homosexual lobby), the media (filled with issues consultants), and compliant legislators ensures that programs are sensitive to homosexuals. The locomotive rolls on and liberationist rhetoric forms a formidable cowcatcher that flips out of the way any isolated moral or political opposition.

Those feelings of loneliness and isolation are not necessary, however, nor is ultimate defeat self-evident. The last decade has shown that groups of citizens can effectively fight this onslaught of homosexual activism. There is no need for negativism. As important as what the homosexuals have done is what they have not done. Among other things, homosexuals have not been able to:

• *Convince Congress to enact civil rights protections for homosexuals equivalent to those provided for racial and other minorities.* Despite the routine introduction of bills attempting to create civil rights protection for homosexuals, spanning over ten years, homosexuals have never been successful in getting those bills out of committee, even with a liberal Congress eager to pass civil rights measures.

• *Eliminate all restrictions on homosexuality in the military, notwithstanding a president who made it a centerpiece of his young administration.* No. The furor of public reaction to President Clinton's *plan,* coupled with staunch opposition both in the military and on Capitol Hill, forced the administration to back down.

• *Convince the Supreme Court that there is a constitutional right to practice consensual sodomy.* To the contrary, the Supreme Court has clearly held that there is no right to commit homosexual sodomy under the Constitution, and that it is perfectly acceptable to criminalize acts of sodomy between consenting adults.

• *Convince the great majority of state legislatures to have state-wide civil rights protection for homosexuals.* Notwithstanding heavily organized homosexual efforts to get states to pass civil rights protection for homosexuals, most have been unsuccessful.

• *Convince most Americans that homosexual behavior is normal and ought to be given special protections.* On nearly every occasion when homosexual rights measures have been put to the voters, they have been resoundingly defeated. Beginning with Dade County, Florida, in 1978, and continuing with the resounding rebuke to a popular governor in an Oregon referendum in 1988 and surprising defeats to homosexual legislation in referendums in Irvine, California, and even San Francisco itself in 1989, the favorable vote on a Colorado initiative in 1992 barring gay rights measures, and more major victories for those opposing gay rights measures in 1993, the voters speak clearly, often overwhelmingly, on this issue.

Fifth, **the key to successful resistance to "gay rights" is an intelligent understanding of the facts.** One factor is preeminent when gay rights measures lose: education. Facts become the ammunition. There is no substitute in any political debate for the intelligent deployment of demonstrable facts. Facts have an impact. Facts work changes. It is typical in political struggles for gay rights proposals to ignite quickly and become popular with both city council members and the public. It is popular to be against "discrimination" and for the provision of "civil rights." Knees jerk predictably when the right political stimulus is given. Good people want to be fair. They do not want to deny anyone, least of all a minority, any rights they might otherwise have. Early polls reflect this bias.

But when citizens educate themselves, and then help educate the general public, the polls change. Minds change. Once the slogans are put aside and the real meaning of gay rights is dispassionately analyzed, gay rights militants are usually put to flight.

The key element, therefore, is to know the facts. Most people opposed to gay rights first react with a instinctive revulsion. Homosexuals call this distaste "homophobia," but it is only the natural revulsion a normal person feels in the face of sexual perversion. Many others react with a moral objection: Homosexual behavior is not right. Or they advance a religious argument: The Bible says homosexuality is wrong. A majority which does not acknowledge the validity of these arguments is often unmoved, and the arguments are easily stigmatized as a moralistic intrusion into the political process. To fight successfully against gay rights proposals, citizens must arm themselves with facts that serve as objective confirmation of their moral reservations about homosexual behavior.

The purpose of this book is to demonstrate that such facts are abundant. Those interested in sound public policy will find overwhelming arguments against giving special privileges to homosexual behavior. The arguments are legal, medical, sociological, economic, and psychological. They are based on facts that belie the slogans and images of homosexual ideology. For those seriously interested in our common welfare, it is necessary to fortify the mind with an abundance of information. Ideas have consequences. Knowledge is power. Truth liberates.

Sixth, **central to understanding the issue of homosexuality is to see both the key arguments of proponents and the reasoned responses of opponents.** This book is organized to facilitate a reasoned response to the most-used arguments of homosexual activists. The argument is firmly stated in bold letters. Then the reasoned response is broken down into several clearly articulated captions that summarize the main points (bold italics). Under each caption, facts are organized and marshaled to provide ammunition for the battle. By reviewing the table of contents and scanning the captions, one can quickly find informed responses to all conventional homosexual arguments.

Those who oppose the abolition of moral norms and wish to promote the special place of the family in American life need to maximize the light shed on this issue.

Light illumines. Light is a natural metaphor for intellectual discovery. Civil rights are important to any American, but their true basis and importance need to be illumined so citizens can be alert to distinguish between true and spurious claims to civil rights protection. Compassion is a Christian virtue, but that virtue needs to be illumined by balancing truths, so that the person who wants to be compassionate can know when that interest is best served by saying yes, and when by saying no.

Light exposes. Jesus talked of people who would not come to light because their deeds were evil. Light exposes the darkness and what is done there. Although there is a natural and wholesome reluctance on the part of decent people to explore the details of deviant behavior, that reluctance must be tempered by a need to give society a common-sense understanding about the nature and public costs of perverted sexual behavior. While the ugliest and most detailed description of perverse acts is well left in darkness, society needs to know which kind of behavior it is being asked to accept as socially legitimate.

Light encourages. As darkness discourages, light encourages. Taking a stand on this issue necessarily requires courage. Those who oppose gay rights measures will often feel like a lightning rod, drawing down on themselves invective, insult, intimidation, even personal threats. To discourage opposition, the well-financed gay rights movement will continue to adopt the air of historical inevitability about their proposals. Proponents know that discouragement paralyzes the opposition.

In the face of this continuing assault, those who believe there are norms for sexual behavior and that "righteousness exalteth a nation," need both courage and good cheer. Because they walk in the light, they need not fear nor apologize for recognizing a difference between the normal and the deviant, the precious and the vile, in sexual expression.

CHAPTER 1

THE AGENDA:
What Homosexuals Really Want

1a. "All we want is tolerance, not approval of our lifestyle. We want to be allowed to be in the mainstream of American life and not be kept on the margins of society."

In reality, homosexuals want complete social acceptance and legal sanction of homosexual behaviors.

Gay rights leaders regularly demonstrate that they want far more than tolerance. They want complete social acceptance. A bit of history will illustrate the increasingly bold objectives of homosexual activists.

During the last two decades, a new group has formed to demand its "rights" and to put an end to "discrimination." The controversy has grown out of a radically new political movement in America, summed up in the slogan "Gay Rights" and dating its formal beginning to June 1969, from a riot at the Stonewall Bar in Greenwich Village in New York City. Before that incident, homosexual political activism had made only fleeting trips out of the closet in American political life. In 1948, there was a "Bachelors for Wallace" group that spoke of organizing those with "our physiological and psychological handicaps...toward the constructive social progress of mankind."[1]

Homosexuals frequently viewed themselves as handicapped prior to the new ideology:

Many of us homosexuals regard our inversion as a handicap because it precludes a complete life. And no life is complete emotionally or biologically without the extension of love and the upbringing of children of one's own.... To boast of being glad for an exclusively homosexual condition is but a defense mechanism.[2]

The 1950s and 1960s saw the appearance of groups such as the Mattachine Society (for male homosexuals) and the Daughters of Bilitis (for lesbians) that edged their way tentatively into the American political scene.[3] In 1961, there was a stir when the first homosexual political candidate, Jose Sarria, ran for city supervisor in San Francisco.[4] But none of these efforts generated significant momentum for the movement, or even widespread attention, until the Stonewall riot.

It started out as a routine police raid on a bar known for illegal sexual behavior. The police arrived, saw what they expected, and began making arrests. But instead of surrendering to police, the patrons fought back with bricks and stones and epithets. The radicalization of America in the late 1960s, with the Yippies, the Weathermen, the Black Panthers, and a host of other groups riding the crest of the anti-war movement, had percolated its way through the homosexual community as well.

The Stonewall resistance was the spark that ignited an explosion of homosexual activism. Homosexuals began to urge that homosexuality not only be tolerated but also accepted as "good, right, and desirable for those who choose to engage in it."[5] The date of the Stonewall riot became "Gay Pride" day, celebrated throughout the United States, often with the blessing of local city councils.

The older homosexual organizations became "Uncle Toms." The new militants became "the children of Christopher Street," and "gay liberation" forces began to link their political agenda to other efforts of rebellion against an allegedly repressive society.

A year later, homosexuals staged an anniversary of the Stonewall riot, demanding the repeal of sodomy laws and mobilizing previously closeted homosexuals into a public demonstration. Homosexuals began verbal assaults against everything from the church to the mass media. Their "book burning" efforts resulted in the successful removal of books not sympathetic to their cause from many university libraries.[6]

Homosexuals were on the march. The most lasting result of the Stonewall riot was thus not a day but a movement. Its goal was, and is, total acceptance of homosexuality. In seeking that end, the movement ran up against two significant social impediments: laws that made homosexual conduct illegal (for example, laws against sodomy), and language that made homosexual conduct unattractive ("sodomy"). A movement aggressively seeking full social acceptance had to clear both hurdles. Laws could be changed only if public perception were changed; public perception could be changed only if language were changed.

1b. "This is all about having the same rights other people do. We're not asking for special preferences."

The ultimate aim of homosexual activists is special protection for their deviant sexual behaviors.

To accomplish their objective, homosexuals now fight tactical battles on three fronts:

1. Where homosexuality is prohibited by law, as in the case of a law prohibiting sodomy, homosexuals seek to repeal those laws or have them declared unconstitutional by the courts.

2. Where there are practices permitted by the law to heterosexuals but not to homosexuals (for example, marriage or adoption of children), homosexuals seek equivalent privileges for themselves.

3. Where the personal discretion or decision-making of individuals impinges on homosexuals (a landlord's choice not to rent

practicing homosexuals a room, for example), homosexuals seek to pass laws that actually create special privileges for homosexual behavior—"gay rights laws" that are not available for people with normal behavior.

Society can take one of three approaches with immoral or socially irresponsible behavior. It can prohibit it (a law against sodomy); it can tolerate it (repeal the law against sodomy or simply not enforce it); it can prefer it (by giving special privileges to those who practice it). It is the third campaign—the fight for special preferences—that homosexuals are now waging in the legislatures, the media, and the schools.

Extending civil rights provisions requires a careful balancing of interests.

On the one hand, a substantial social benefit is derived in continuing the historic deference given to human choices and discretion. The freedom of association valued by all Americans includes a corollary right to non-association. On the other hand, there is also a strong social benefit in discouraging arbitrary decisions that cause widespread injury to innocent parties. Human rights laws have struck a delicate balance that accommodates both interests. They give substantial relief to those who have been the victims of prejudice, but they do so without limiting the right of anyone to make decisions based on any reasonable criteria. By forbidding arbitrary or irrational decisions that cause substantial harm to innocent parties, human rights laws preserve intact discretionary decision-making based on reason and common sense.

Homosexuals already have the same basic constitutional rights everyone enjoys.

Homosexuals have all the same rights heterosexuals do. They are protected by the Bill of Rights,[7] by federal and state statutes,[8] and by common-law decisions.[9] They have the same status before the law as do other citizens. Yet through gay rights ordinances, they demand to join the few classes of citizens having characteristics immune from scrutiny. The issue is not whether rights have been infringed; the issue is whether new rights, not previously recognized, should be created.

To understand an issue, one must correctly define it.

The real issue underlying the gay rights controversy is whether the law should give special protection for homosexual behavior. Does the inclination to practice anal or oral sodomy (or related sexual practices) with members of the same sex merit special legal safeguards?

The public policy issue is straightforward. A group of citizens, bound together by common sexual taste, comes seeking insulation of their sexual behavior from scrutiny by other members of society; they want, in short, to debar others from taking sexual orientation or behavior into account in making social decisions. They seek the privilege of having one aspect of their behavior eliminated as a criterion for exercising a general right to associate, or dissociate, with others.

Much of the debate about such political claims leaves underlying presuppositions unanalyzed. Among them is the presupposition that everyone has a preexisting right to protect his preferences and predispositions from being taken into account by other people. Referring to "gay rights" as "civil rights" is begging the question—it assumes such rights exist. With that assumption in place, the only question that remains is, have those rights been infringed? Has there been discrimination? Once discrimination has been shown, it follows that wrong should give rise to remedy. The remedy is explicit civil rights protections for homosexuals.

Homosexual activists are adept at using language to disguise their true agenda. Correct definition of issues must not be diverted by the emotive power of language.

The gay rights controversy shows the mystifying power of language to forge a consensus. The homosexuals' use of clever expressions to convey a hidden meaning has been well explored by various writers. To be "compassionate" means to accept homosexual behavior. A "stable, loving relationship" means that homosexual pairings are equivalent to marriage. "Stereotyping" means it is irrational to assume that all homosexual practices are wrong. "Sexual minority" suggests that homosexuals are a legitimate minority. All such expressions are designed to put nonhomosexuals on the defensive.

The language of such laws is simple on its face. Most gay rights ordinances forbid "discrimination" in housing, employment, and public accommodations based on a person's "affectional or sexual preference" or "affectional or sexual orientation."[10]

While the words make fine political slogans, they evade clear political analysis. Homosexuals use language to distort the real issues. They seek to use techniques George Orwell described in his "Politics and the English Language." He showed that language is not a servile handmaiden of political debate. Indeed, it often calls the shots. Language shapes, defines, motivates, and in large measure determines the answer in political debate by the way it states the question. To think clearly on an issue, one must precisely define it. In this arena as in all others, Orwell pointed out, clear thinking requires clear language. The "slovenliness of our language," he said, "makes it easier for us to have foolish thoughts." If "one gets rid of these habits, one can think more clearly, and to think clearly is a necessary first step to political regeneration."[11]

Political pollsters have long known this relationship. Most people do not favor "abortion on demand." On the other hand, most people are against taking away a woman's "constitutional right" to "control her own body" or to "terminate a pregnancy." Curiously, many people can be lured into contradictory positions simply by the pollster's choice of words. They are for "reproductive freedom" and for the "rights of unborn children." Few people want, in their heart of hearts, to be either "anti-choice" or "anti-life."

Words used in political debate frequently carry heavy emotional baggage. It is virtually impossible for anyone to rise up against offering any group of people their rights. It is equally impossible to be in favor of discrimination. Rights are as American as Abraham Lincoln; discrimination is a black person trudging silently to the back of the bus. Yet such terms more often confuse than illuminate homosexual issues. There are rights whose creation nearly everyone agrees would threaten the continued existence of society: the right to steal, to mug, to refuse to pay taxes. There are forms of discrimination that serve as the foundation of a just system of law. Indeed, why is a person of good judgment called "discriminating"? Every person, no matter what his role, must exercise wise discretion in life, and discretion presupposes a range of available options from which one tries to choose the best or avoid the worst. The judge, in his discretion, must determine whether the plaintiff or the defendant has the better claims and treat him accordingly. The employer, in his discretion, must determine who among his employees is the most diligent and who deserves a raise in pay or quick advancement. The wise shopper discriminates in the choice of products at the supermarket.

The proper place of discrimination is apparent. The problem is that homosexuals want total acceptance and social sanction for their chosen behaviors with no evaluation of those behaviors and their consequences to society.

That homosexuals want preferred status before the law is shown by their hysterical opposition to laws that simply prohibit preferences or protection based on sexual behavior. Colorado Amendment 2, which is now tied up in the Colorado court system and is often described as a hateful Neo-Nazi proposal, is really a sensible and even-handed measure:

> Neither the State of Colorado, through any of its branches or departments, nor any of its agencies, political subdivision, municipalities or school districts, shall enact, adopt or enforce any statute, regulation, ordinance or policy whereby homosexual, lesbian or bi-sexual orientation, conduct, practices or relationships shall constitute or otherwise be the basis of or

entitle any person or class of persons to have or claim any
minority status quota preferences, protected status or claim of
discrimination.[12]

**1c. "We have no secret agenda. We simply
want to be treated like other people."**

*A review of published demands of homosexual groups shows how
extensive their agenda really is.*

The lack of any compelling necessity and the homosexuals'
attempt to squeeze into an ill-fitting niche (oppressed minority group),
suggest that gay rights laws are not the objective, but are simply a
weigh station en route to what homosexuals really want: full social
acceptance. The true nature of the movement's goals was made clear
more than two decades ago, as revealed in a review of homosexual
demands comprising the various planks of the 1972 Gay Rights
Platform:[13]

Federal:

- Amend all federal Civil Rights acts, other legislation, and
government controls to prohibit discrimination in employment, housing, public accommodations, and public services.

- Issuance by the president of an executive order prohibiting the
military from excluding for reasons of their sexual orientation,
persons who…desire entrance into the Armed Services; and
from issuing less-than-fully-honorable discharges for homosexuality; and the upgrading to fully honorable all such discharges previously issued, with retroactive benefits.

- Federal encouragement and support for sex education courses,
prepared and taught by gay women and men, presenting
homosexuality as a valid, healthy preference and lifestyle as a
viable alternative to heterosexuality.

- Federal funding of aid programs of gay men's and women's organizations designed to alleviate the problems encountered by gay women and men which are engendered by an oppressive sexist society.

- Immediate release of all gay women and men now incarcerated...because of sexual offense charges related to victimless crimes or sexual orientation; and that adequate compensation be made for the physical and mental duress encountered; and that all existing records relating to the incarceration be immediately expunged.

State:

- Repeal of all state laws prohibiting private sexual acts involving consenting persons; equalization for homosexuals and heterosexuals for the enforcement of all laws.

- Repeal of all state laws prohibiting solicitation for private voluntary sexual liaisons; and laws prohibiting prostitution, both male and female.

- Enactment of legislation so that child custody, adoption, visitation rights, foster parenting, and the like shall not be denied because of sexual orientation or marital status.

- Repeal of all laws governing the age of sexual consent.

- Repeal of all legislative provisions that restrict the sex or number of persons entering into a marriage unit; and the extension of legal benefits to all persons who cohabit regardless of sex or numbers.

The militants are far closer to these objectives today than in 1972. And this is just the beginning of their demands.

Education is a front considered vital by homosexual groups and a front on which they are very active.

Homosexual teachers in New York City have come out in support of the right of a teacher to have sex with a boy so long as it occurs outside the school.[14] The Gay Teachers Association has called for "A Bill of Rights for Gay Teachers and Students,"[15] which makes the following demands:

A BILL OF RIGHTS FOR GAY TEACHERS AND STUDENTS

We, the members of the Gay Teachers Association, proud of our gay heritage and lifestyle, and believing strongly in the principles of free speech, the right to life, liberty, and the pursuit of happiness, and in the duty of gay people to strike out against bigotry and ignorance on every level, do herein:

- Affirm our civil rights so that our right to work is ensured
- Affirm the beauty and legitimacy of our lifestyle
- Affirm the role of gay educators throughout history
- Affirm our rights to educate all people about the outstanding contributions of gay writers, gay painters, gay historians, gay psychologists, sociologists, philosophers, and a host of other gay people who have invested their talents in the culture of a world society
- Affirm the rights of gay students to non-judgmental information and counseling
- Affirm that gay is proud.

And in so affirming we set forth the following demands:

- We demand that the board of education include in the preamble of its contract with our union the phrase "sexual orientation" in its listing of nondiscriminatory practices
- We demand that our union and all its affiliates work actively to see to it that this phrase be included in our contract
- We demand that the principle of academic freedom be supported for gay teachers so that they need not fear affirming their sexual preference nor fear correcting misinformation which might occur in or out of the classroom

- We demand all these things so that the cycle of oppression of gay people, oppression which stifles creativity, which stifles positive self-images, can be terminated.

In a paper called "Lesbians and the Schools," Jean O'Leary, a prominent lesbian appointed by Jimmy Carter to the National Commission for the Observance of International Women's Year, demands that schools offer sex education courses "to encourage students to explore alternative lifestyles, including lesbianism," that school libraries be stocked with books extolling homosexuals, that homosexual clubs be established in schools to foster a community spirit among homosexuals, and that books that disparage homosexuality be banned. In addition, she recommends that students be furnished with names of homosexual counseling services available in the community and that teachers of "human sexuality courses" take a "positive view" of homosexuality.[16]

The 1993 homosexual demonstration in Washington hit many of the same themes. Among the "Platform Demands" of the Lesbian, Gay and Bisexual 1993 March on Washington were:

1. Elimination of all laws prohibiting sodomy, transgendered expression (cross-dressing) and sadomasochism (§1.04).

2. Lowering the age-of-consent for homosexual and heterosexual sex (§1.08).

3. Implementation of homosexual, bisexual and transgendered curriculum at all levels of education (§4.02).

4. Legalization of homosexual marriages (§3.07).

5. Custody, adoption and foster care rights for homosexuals, lesbians, and transgendered people; redefinition of family to include the full diversity of all family structures (§3.01).

6. Access to all programs of the Boy Scouts of America (§7.05).

7. Affirmative action for homosexuals and lesbians (§6.02).

8. Inclusion of sex-change operations under a universal health care plan (§2.12 & §2.01).

9. Abortion on demand for all people, without restriction and regardless of age (§5.05).

10. A national needle exchange program (§2.10).[17]

As registered above, the homosexual agenda is pervasive. It is also in many ways a "secret agenda." Most normal Americans have no knowledge of what the homosexual activist is vying for.

Homosexuals use civil rights theory as a lever to get affirmative action.

The move for gay rights also bears with it the possibility of increasing demands for affirmative action, using the successes of the civil rights movement generally as a model. Already, homosexual activists have sought quotas in certain areas. The task force on the status of lesbian and gay male psychologists of the American Psychological Association, for example, demanded that "all panels on homosexuality (at national and regional meetings) shall include at least one member of the Association of Gay Psychologists as a panel member, and all paper sessions (at national and regional meetings) shall include at least one member of the Association of Gay Psychologists to serve as a discussant."[18]

Homosexuals increasingly seek preferred treatment on the university campus.

At a number of universities, those staff and faculty who co-habit with same-sex partners get higher priority than heterosexual couples. At Stanford, for example, homosexuals receive as their reward higher priority for housing, health, and other family-related benefits than do heterosexual university employees. In the *Report of the University Subcommittee on Domestic Partners Benefits,* the preference for sodomy seemed non-controversial:

> The subcommittee is unanimous in the view that the case for extending benefits to heterosexual partners is weaker than for

gay and lesbian partners. As a result, the subcommittee recommends that if current cost considerations militate against
extending coverage to both groups, coverage be extended
now to gays and lesbians, and the question of coverage for
heterosexual partners be considered at a later date.[19]

One professor was offended by the possibility of including heterosexuals. He sniffed, "the inclusion of opposite-sex domestic partners...dilutes the symbolism of this report."[20]

*Homosexual militants seek to remove long-standing laws prohibiting
sodomy.*

One long-term goal of the homosexual movement has been to
repeal laws prohibiting sodomy. Although gay rights activists have
concentrated on promoting gay rights ordinances, they have not abandoned their attack on existing sodomy statutes. As long as their behavior remains criminal, it is hard for them to argue that they deserve special protection for it. When challenging sodomy statutes, homosexuals
argue that there is a "right to privacy" in the Constitution that protects
private acts of consensual sodomy.

*The demand for social acceptance leads ultimately to demands for
same-sex marriage.*

In November 1993, there was a marriage at Stanford's Memorial
Church. The names of the couple "married" were Jason Allen and
Terry Rouman. Both are men. The associate dean of the church, Diane
Akiyama, performed the ceremony with the blessing of her husband,
the dean of students. Undeterred by expressions of outrage by those
who felt it to be a sacrilege, Dean Akiyama proudly promised more. It
was done in such a way, the dean said, that it would be obvious to
non-homosexuals that it was "equal to their weddings." This reflects
the recent priority given by those who want to "empower" homosexual partnerships by providing the same benefits given to heterosexual
marriage. By explicit social policy, married couples receive significant

legal benefits. They can file joint tax returns, inherit property, use gift and estate tax mechanisms to maximize their estate, bring wrongful death actions on behalf of a spouse, and enjoy a host of other benefits. Homosexuals want the same benefits for their frequently transitory relationships.[21]

Several jurisdictions are considering domestic partnership legislation. Indeed, the Court of Appeals for the State of New York held in 1989 that a "domestic partnership" of two male homosexuals was the equivalent of marriage. The historic concept of marriage could be stretched to include homosexuals because the court found the idea of marriage to be a legal fiction. Gay rights laws can be used as a foot in the door to such social experimentation. If discrimination against homosexuals is wrong, why not let them marry?

In fact, a major thrust of the homosexual rights movement will increasingly be to validate homosexual marriage. It is the final legitimation of homosexual behavior. "Homosexual marriage" is, of course, an oxymoron. It is a contradiction that makes no sense, lexically or legally. The word *marriage* itself means "the institution whereby men and women are joined in a special kind of social and legal dependence, for the purpose of founding and maintaining a family" (*Webster's New International Dictionary*).

Legally, homosexual marriage is also a confusion. As Justice Harlan pointed out nearly thirty years ago, "the intimacy of husband and wife [unlike relations based on homosexuality, fornication, and incest] is necessarily an essential and accepted feature of the institution of marriage." Justice Harlan's position, nearly identical to that expressed by Thomas Jefferson two centuries earlier, is well taken. The harsh reality is that all forms of sexual expression are not equally normal. Simulating a family is not being a family.

In addition, while a truly monogamous marriage is a relationship without venereal diseases and attendant spill-over costs to society, abnormal sex translates into substantial public expense. And once the bright line of exclusivity attached to heterosexual marriage is crossed, where will society stop? Will special privileges be given to those who by reason of culture, inclination, or private choice seek sexual outlet in polygamy, incest, or communal groupings?

This confused thinking always leads to bizarre twists, as was illustrated by a controversy in the United Church of Christ in 1993. A female pastor was under threat of discipline in Wisconsin. A lesbian, who had lesbian lovers while pastoring the church, had now committed a less pardonable sin. She had fallen in love with a man and abandoned a lesbian lifestyle. Her formal charge was related to having relations with the man with no marriage license; her lesbian sexual encounters triggered no such discipline.[22]

Every small homosexual victory is another chip acquired in a much larger game.

Mike Royko sums up the focus of the homosexual agenda well in commenting on the issue of homosexuals in the military in the *Chicago Tribune*:

> If gays are accepted by the military, they will demand change. Some activists will probably push for a gay quota at West Point.

> There's nothing wrong with change if it has a positive purpose. This doesn't. We're not talking about patriotism, love of country, sacrifice. Gay obsessives—not to be confused with ordinary people who happen to be gay—have an agenda: total social acceptance. And they are using the military ban as a blue chip in their poker game.[23]

1d. "Don't blame us for the demands of some fringe activists or extremists. All we want is what you already have."

If homosexual activists want the law to protect a constituency, they must be prepared for an examination of who that constituency is and what it does.

The question is: Whom do you seek to protect, merely that rarest of endangered species, the monogamous homosexual? Or do you seek to protect homosexuals who march alongside you in gay pride rallies? If you are a movement of many constituencies, should we not examine the components of your movement?

Groups like the North American Man/Boy Love Association (NAMBLA) is carrying the ideology of the homosexual movement to its natural conclusion. If there is no such thing as perversion and if sex is good, the exercise of the merely physical appetite, then why should children be denied this good?

A Boston University professor, one of the most prominent veterans of the movement, recently underscored this attitude when he called for a $25 fine as the maximum penalty for sex with minors.

Homosexual demonstrations reveal the composition of the movement.

A look at the participants in a "gay pride" march reveals the constituents of the movement and outlines of the slippery slope in evidence once the guardrails of morality from sex and conduct are removed. At what point can one say no to sexual deviants? As one commentator pointed out:

Homosexual activists would have us believe that they're just ordinary people like the rest of us, with no particular fixation on sex and sexuality. Is this claim valid?

Well, judge for yourself. A recent festival of bisexual, gay, and lesbian life at the University of Chicago featured the following events:

- a condom distribution on the main quad;
- "French Your Way to Your B.A.: Queer Theory Kissing Booth;"

- a workshop on "Eroticizing Safe Sex;"
- a "Dyke Fashion Show;"
- "Sex in Public: 'Family Values' in the Public Sphere" (brunch and panel discussion).

Sounds pretty bizarre, huh? I'll pass on that brunch.[24]

CHAPTER 2

THE APPROACH:
*Take the Offensive and Stay Away
from the Behavior*

2a. "We should show sensitivity to gay men and lesbians in their quest for dignity and basic civil rights."

Use of common buzz words is no substitute for serious analysis.

Framing the issue in such "buzz words" foreshadows how distorting the meaning of language will lead to distortions in public policy. "Sensitivity" and "quests" and "dignity" and "basic rights" and "diversity" are all good things. Lagard Smith, a law professor at Pepperdine, shows the subtle bias introduced into the debate by referring to the "gay community." Community is a positive thing, evoking thoughts of the American small town. Linking community to "gay" is an attempt to have some of the good feeling rub off.[1] One sees the effect by substituting other deviant behavior. How about the "Alcoholic Community," the "White Collar Crime Community," or the "Wife-Swapper Community"? While, as Smith acknowledges, there is a community of interest among those drawn together by sexual behaviors, it is hardly a community in the traditional sense of the term.

But the homosexual militant is not talking about "community" or sensitivity to moral norms, to right and wrong. He is not talking about the quest for dignity that organizes people into stable families and makes sacrificial investments in the next generation. He is not promoting the basic right to associate with people of high moral purpose. And he certainly is not calling for diversity in opinion about homosexuality—only one view is correct there. No, what the "buzz" homosexuals want to leave with their listeners is a "feeling," not a rational analysis. By obscuring the real issue of the controversy they have a better chance at achieving their political agenda.

Put plainly, gay rights laws are meant to protect men and women who practice oral and anal copulation with members of the same sex. In about half the states, their behavior violates criminal laws. In a televised debate, a questioner asked the head of a local human rights agency whether she thought there was really no moral difference between giving special protection to people of good character who happened to have been born black and giving special protection to men who made a voluntary choice to commit sodomy with other men. "Why," she blurted out, "gays would never do that."[2] Such is the "buzz" that the power of language can create.

Homosexuals seek to equate genuine minority status with sexual behavior.

In the last two decades, gay rights activists have begun to press a new, radically different set of claims to civil rights protection. Human rights statutes historically have granted special legal standing to those "discrete and insular minorities" who share an immutable *status*.[3] That status was generally unrelated to behavior, traditional perceptions of moral character, or public health. One's racial inheritance, for example, creates a true *status*. Race tells us nothing about a person's lifestyle or behavior. Removing race as a criterion of social decision-making therefore makes sense to all but the most arbitrary decision-maker.

Gay rights proposals redefine status without ever saying so. Rather than acknowledge that such laws protect a social behavior (say, the commission of anal sodomy), the benefits or detriments of which to society must be objectively evaluated before the protection is given, proponents create a new minority status. An uncritical acceptance of that new status derails a rational inquiry into the underlying behavior and disguises the fact that this minority is bound together by sexual activity—a common inclination to commit sodomy with members of the same sex. This new status group, given a new name ("gay"), which itself begs the question of whether the group shares a common nature or a common behavior, has been proposed as worthy of legal protection under human rights laws extended to include "sexual preference" or "sexual orientation."

As Dennis Prager says, homosexuals "are not a persecuted minority in the same way that, let us say, blacks have been. Sexual lifestyle is qualitatively different from skin color."[4]

2b. "We need to do something to stop gay bashing!"

Condemning gay-bashing is a red herring. No serious spokesman on either side of the controversy is in favor of such violence, and it is already against the law in every state.

Homosexuals use "gay-bashing" incidents as proof that they need special legal protection. While these arguments are often effective, since they connect with the emotions of any audience, arousing a natural sense of indignation, they do little to illuminate the real issues, because:

a. Such incidents are already against the law in every jurisdiction of the country. Such offenses, whether styled as assault or battery or mayhem, are treated seriously by courts and trigger significant penalties.

b. To suggest that those who oppose gay rights laws support mugging or personal abuse of homosexuals is, of course, utterly unfair. No one can seriously claim, much less substantiate, that offenses against homosexuals are somehow orchestrated or silently supported by people who oppose special privileges for homosexual behavior.

c. The perpetrators of such offenses, skinheads and toughs heading home from the bars, are the same kind of people who are a danger to *all* citizens out after dark. They are terrifying to law-abiding citizens of every kind, since the combination of alcohol and assaultive tendencies increasingly threatens everyone in our cities.

Extreme homosexual activists are the principal practitioners of organized violence and intimidation on this issue.

While there are no organized attacks on homosexuals by heterosexual groups with political aims, there are an increasing number of assaults by militant homosexuals on people who oppose their political aims. These groups, whether Act Up chapters or a number of related organizations, have engaged in a variety of assaultive acts over the past few years. In October 1993, a large group of homosexuals stormed Hamilton Square Baptist Church in San Francisco. The church was preparing for a Sunday evening service, which featured the head of a traditional values coalition, sponsored by thousands of California churches. When the staff heard that some trouble might be brewing, it called the police, who seemed uninterested in the reports, saying, "After all, this is San Francisco." In the hour before the service, rampaging homosexuals vandalized the property, throwing a bench into a fountain outside the church, pounded on walls and doors, and surrounded elderly people trying to get into the church, leaving them terrified as they became unable to move. Lesbians mocked parishioners by showing off their breasts to them. Only after the arrival of riot police was the mob brought under control, and the pastor and speaker safely escorted off the premises.

This incident, like others catalogued elsewhere in this book, is reminiscent of the conduct of crowds in Sodom, and the Benjamite affair described in the book of Judges. The difference between these frightening displays of mob intimidation and the gay-bashing complained of by homosexuals is evident: The former are random acts of bullying that can happen to anyone; the latter are organized groups seeking to carry out political objectives.

2c. "But for your homophobia, you would see our side, too. You seem to be fascinated by sex and sleaze and have used all kinds of false and distorted information. I am disappointed that you manifest such homophobia, hate mongering, and bigotry."

Homosexual activists use name-calling and personal attacks but avoid talking about the real issues.

"Homophobia" is a convenient slur on those who disagree with any part of the homosexual agenda. It should be dealt with for what it is:

a. Can we agree to have a civilized discussion on these important issues and not resort to name-calling? Can we look at whether granting special protection to practitioners of one type of sex makes sense and leave the slogans and personal attacks out of the discussion?

b. We are not dealing with phobias here but with facts. Anyone with an ounce of compassion would be concerned about the very real consequences of a homosexual lifestyle. *Any behavior that has a majority of its adherents dying before fifty should be regarded with some concern.*

c. Why don't people call this sort of thing McCarthyism anymore? Can I oppose special protection for incest without being incestophobic? For adultery without being adulterophobic? For bestiality without being beastophobic? What the gay rights militants are doing, of course, is branding their opponents, a majority of the American public, with being crazy or sick or both, if they disagree with the homosexual agenda.

d. Is it possible that a distaste for same-sex sodomy may be instinctive and altogether natural? Is homophobia the natural revulsion normal people feel in the face of sexual perversion? Is this the kind of feeling one has for incest or child molestation?

e. While homosexuals tar their opponents with name-calling, they are vulnerable to the same thing. What do John Gacy, Wayne Williams, Juan Corona, Jeffrey Dahmer, and Elmer Henley have in common, besides being serial killers? They were all "gay." One could imagine the kind of hysteria that would be generated in the media and by supporters of the homosexual agenda if these social misfits were members of the "religious right."[5]

As Prager points out:

> Just as we owe homosexuals humane, decent, and respectful conduct, homosexuals owe the same to the rest of us. Homosexuals' use of the term "homophobic," however, violates this rule as much as heterosexuals' use of the term "faggot" does.

> When the term "homophobic" is used to describe anyone who believes that heterosexuality should remain Western society's ideal, it is quite simply a contemporary form of McCarthyism. In fact, it is more insidious than the late senator's use of "communist." For one thing, there was and is such a thing as a communist. But "homophobia" masquerades as a scientific description of a phobia that does not exist in any medical list of phobias.[6]

There is nothing "bigoted" or "homophobic" about carefully evaluating a group that asks for special legal privileges.

It is not "homophobic" to call attention to homosexual behavior. To understand the gay rights issue, it is necessary to describe the lifestyle of the modern homosexual. Much of the statistical data is available from surveys done by homosexuals themselves. The bizarre practices that they disclose, including some of the more extreme and eccentric behaviors, show the kinds of activity given special protection by gay rights legislation.

In describing homosexual behavior, of course, it is necessary to generalize. There are homosexual men and women who are less promiscuous than average, who seldom (or never) engage in sexual practices in public places, who practice less exotic forms of perversion, and who live relatively conventional lives. Conversely, there are homosexual men and women who are more promiscuous than average. Wherever they may fall in the continuum of homosexual experience, however, these people are entitled to all the freedoms and protections of our system of law without exception.

Homosexuals are made, not born. They are responsible for their conduct. But no person of good will should use this as a justification for personal acts of cruelty, violence, or insult. On a personal as well as legal basis, homosexuals are entitled to respect as human beings, as persons with immortal souls. But this respect does not require the provision of special privileges that would infringe on the rights or liberties of others, nor that we ignore behaviors that are destructive to society and homosexuals themselves. A concern for homosexuals as people will lead, paradoxically, to examining their behavior and withholding social acceptance from those who practice it.

2d. "No one chooses to be a homosexual or can be 'recruited' into this lifestyle. Do you think anyone would choose to suffer like we do?"

The number of people experimenting with homosexual sodomy is influenced by social attitudes toward such behavior.

The social acceptance gay rights laws give to homosexual behavior creates a climate in which opportunities for homosexual behavior multiply. As the restraints of law and public morality dissolve and homosexuality becomes publicly celebrated as a valid lifestyle, it is logical to expect more people to explore the practice. More latent homosexuals will find opportunities for overt behavior, and with that overt behavior will go the inevitable consequences.

Many homosexuals talk about recruiting apparent "straights" into homosexual behavior.[7] This influence can savage the person ensnared who, at a different time, may never have been at risk in the first place.

The simple fact is that the more public expressions of perversion there are, the more likely one is to experiment with it. Tastes become more jaded as each new moral barrier is broken through. The poster child of this degeneracy is Hugh Hefner. Having hurdled a number of moral barriers in his life, he thought to try homosexual relations. He engaged in sodomy with other men.

> The founder of the *Playboy* magazine and clubs, and self-styled Father of the Sexual Revolution, said: "I was exploring the outer limits of my own sexuality and it included bisexuality."
>
> Bunnies and Playmates spread themselves over his glossy color pages, and staffed his nightclubs. They also hopped in and out of his fabled "console" bed, fitted with everything from drink coolers to television screens.
>
> But his image of the man who had everything was based on the premise that what he had was young, blonde, bronzed, leggy—and, of course, female.
>
> Now he tells *Details* that he agrees with Freud—the father, surely, of sexual neuroses—that all men are born bisexual.
>
> But his former followers will be relieved to hear that he discovered at the outer limits of his sexuality that he preferred girls.[8]

Prager makes the point well:

> Wherever homosexuality has been encouraged, far more people have engaged in it. And wherever heterosexuality has been discouraged, homosexuality has similarly flourished, as, for example, in prisons and elsewhere: As Greenberg has written, "High levels of homoeroticism develop in boarding schools, monasteries, isolated rural regions, and on ships with all-male crews."[9]

Some homosexuals, especially lesbians, consciously choose a homosexual lifestyle as a political affirmation.

The fact is borne out by lesbians who turn to their lifestyle more to make a political statement than as a result of attraction:

Each of us who loves another woman has grown up in a sexist society which devalues women and fails to give us a strong sense of identity.

Butch-femme relationships can become dangerously close to perpetuating sexism and oppressive heterosexual models.

As lesbians we have a chance to move away from male defined sexuality.

When I'm having troubles with a man and tell a lesbian friend, she usually gets a look in her eye which means, "What did you expect, being with a man?"[10]

Charlotte Bunch, an editor of *Lesbians and the Women's Movement,* said:

Lesbianism is the key to liberation and only women who cut their ties to male privilege can be trusted to remain serious in the struggle against male dominance.[11]

Jill Johnson wrote the same in her book, "The continued collusion of any woman with any man is an event that retards the progress of women's supremacy."[12]

2e. "Call us by our name. We are gay people."

While through politeness one may call people by the names they have chosen, it is important not to be misled by labels that obscure the nature or practices of the group.

While some homosexuals like the shock therapy of calling themselves "queers" and "fairies," most male homosexuals call themselves *gays.* Female homosexuals frequently refer to themselves as *lesbians,* based on the alleged sexual practices of women on the isle of Lesbos.

Although nomenclature changes somewhat from place to place,

the conventional terminology is "gay men and lesbian women." *Gay* is used to suggest a cheerful, free, and sunny approach to life. *Lesbian* suggests something more assertive and masculine. Both project a consciously chosen identity, putting a more positive face on the respective groups than the taunting language of the street. Neither deals honestly with the underlying sexual behavior.

The same intent is behind the use of the terms *affectional preference* or *sexual orientation*. To be affectionate is an unqualified good, as warm and comfortable as a good lap dog. We like to receive and to give affection. To interrupt the affection two people have for one another comes off as a Scrooge-like interference in wholesome and humane relationships. The same is true of preferences. In a tolerant society, a gentleman always recognizes another's preferences. "Coffee—cream or sugar?" "Do you take tea with lemon, sir?" "Do you prefer it a little cooler?" asks the bellhop. Sexual orientation, on the other hand, suggests a predisposition or inclination that is both neutral and natural.

Traditional terms for homosexual behavior often lead to a more clear analysis of what is at stake.

To see how language prejudges the issue, we need merely substitute some synonyms. Take, for example, the English equivalent. In England, what homosexuals do together is called *buggery*, both in law and on the street. Imagine a group calling for "buggers' rights" or speaking of "buggers' pride." The American equivalent in legal language is *sodomy*, defined generally as unnatural sexual relations, especially between male persons or between a human being and an animal. Imagine, if you will, a call for "sodomites' rights." To understand who is seeking protection, it is important to look beyond the terms *gay* and *affectional preference*, beyond images of men strolling together along the seashore of Greek islands thinking great thoughts and displaying tender affection—in short, beyond the language to get to an understanding of the group seeking protection.

2f. "We have to make it unlawful for people to use hate speech against minorities. The paradox is this: We have no free speech right ourselves unless hate speech is banned."

Homosexual militants frequently use "doublespeak" to justify censorship of different opinions on homosexuality.

Again the approach is Orwellian. "Free speech" means censored speech. Liberation means taking away the liberty of association. Banning of "hate speech" means we can use hate speech against those who oppose our agenda.

Homosexuals want to make illegal the demeaning of a sexual orientation. Several gay rights laws include provisions making it unlawful to "deride" or "denigrate" homosexual status. While these laws are explained as an effort to discourage the taunting of homosexuals, their application is more far-reaching and could include criminal penalties for ministers who express from the pulpit the view that homosexual acts are shameful. To the extent such laws merely proscribe "terroristic threats," they add nothing to laws already in existence that make such threats illegal, regardless of the sexual orientation of the victim.

But these ordinances go further. An ordinance before the Seattle City Council would have made it illegal to "discredit, demoralize, or belittle another person by words or conduct" based on sexual orientation.[13] Such hate-crime measures have been introduced in Congress. A Seattle prosecutor commented it would be a "new tool" in his arsenal. The tool is unfortunately so blunt that it could be used against those who "belittle" or "discredit" homosexuals by calling sodomy perverted or sinful. One Swedish pastor was sentenced to jail for preaching a sermon from Romans 1 that was found to be belittling to homosexuals. Interestingly, groups historically identified with free speech, such as the American Civil Liberties Union (ACLU), support laws that could restrict the freedom to express deeply rooted religious convictions. Gay rights laws are but a step on the way to such destinations.

No one is helped by name-calling. No serious people defend it. But homosexuals use it against others and adopt names for themselves that advance their cause.

Calls for diversity usually mean: We encourage every kind of diversity except diversity of opinion.

The homosexual militants are really antagonistic to free speech. The talk of diversity obscures the censorship that goes on in the name of gay rights:

a.   "Diversity" means that all are welcome if they think the same on this issue. Diversity is not diversity if every color, nationality, and sexual preference is there; it occurs only if they all think the same! Most diversity programs seek to "educate" the audience with a particular view of homosexuality that is often far removed from the realities of homosexual experience. Those who object are browbeaten into silence by being called homophobic, or worse.

b.   Homosexuals have enthusiastically endorsed speech codes that forbid saying anything "not accepting" of the homosexual lifestyle.

c.   The homosexual militant is comfortable with the language of blame. All of the problems of homosexuals, all the diseases, unhappiness and irresponsibility are caused by the ignorance and hatred of others.

2g. "You are Nazis at heart. They persecuted homosexuals, too."

Nazis who persecuted homosexuals were part of a movement that had many sexual deviants in it.

While Hitler's storm troopers did persecute and harass homosexuals, it is well known that sexual perversion was a significant diversion, if not obsession, among Nazi leaders themselves. As Ludwig Lenz put it in commenting on the destruction of the Institute of Sexology in 1933, founded by the homosexual Magnus Hirschfeld, and of which Lenz was a part:

> Whence this hatred, and what was even more strange, this haste and thoroughness? The answer to this is simple and straightforward enough—we knew too much. It would be against medical principles to provide a list of the Nazi leaders and their perversions. One thing, however, is certain—not ten percent of those men who in 1933 took the fate of Germany into their hands was sexually normal...."[14]

Some close Hitler associates were homosexuals.

In *Germany's National Vice,*[15] the author notes that Adolf Hitler surrounded himself with homosexuals, like Hess, Roehm, and a variety of other lieutenants in the storm troopers. He says:

> In light of the mass murders carried out by Hitler's orders on June 30, 1934, it showed that the destinies of Germany, and therewith the peace of Europe, were at the mercy of a pathological criminal who was surrounded by a group of sexual perverts like himself.[16]

While this does nothing to debunk the clear evidence that homosexuals were arrested, suffered, and sometimes perished in concentration camps, it does show the presence of sexual perversion and other forms of immorality in Nazi Germany.

CHAPTER 3

THE AUTHENTICATION:

Why It Is Important for Homosexuals to Misrepresent Who and How Many They Are (and Were)

3a. "We represent ten percent, perhaps fifteen percent, of the population. How can you deny us our rights?".

The long-standing claim of the homosexual movement that ten to fifteen percent of society is homosexual has been repeatedly shown to be false.

A representative of the American Psychological Association (APA), Bryant Welch, boldly made this claim in an appearance before the American Bar Association: An "orientation [to homosexuality is] found consistently in about ten percent of the male population and approximately five percent of the female population." And "across different historical eras and in totally different cultures the incidence of homosexuality remained the same.'"[1] His claim is utterly false. A long-time favorite in the gay rights arsenal of propaganda, it has been widely disproved, and never was supported by a credible study to begin with.

A few examples of modern research shows a clear pattern:

- Of 6,300 randomly drawn Norwegians in 1987, 0.9% of the men and 0.9% of the women reported homosexual sex in the past 3 years; 3.5% of the men and 3.0% of the women claimed a homosexual experience at some time in their life, including adolescent experimentation.[2]

- A 1989 Danish survey of 3,178 randomly drawn adults reported that fewer than 3% of the men claimed to be bisexual or homosexual and 2.7% said that they had had at least one homosexual experience in their lifetime.[3]

- In a 1989-1990 British survey of 2,171 youths aged 16 to 20 years of age, 2.5% of the males and 2.4% of the females reported ever having had a homosexual experience.[4]

- The National Opinion Research Center did a questionnaire of 904 U.S. men of age 21 or over in 1989 and 1990. Only 1.3% reported sex with men in the past year.[5]

- In a study of 36,741 Minnesota public school students in 1986 and 1987, fewer than 2% of the boys and fewer than 2% of the girls claimed to be bisexual or homosexual.[6]

- In one survey done by Thomas Coates and John Gagnon with a team of other sex researchers, it was revealed that approximately 2% of the population had had any homosexual encounter. The study was done as a result of national random-digit dialing in which 13,785 adults between 18 and 75 were telephoned.[7]

- An anonymous exit poll taken by a consortium of ABC, CBS, NBC, and CNN found only 2.4% of respondents saying they are gay, lesbian, or bisexual. A comment on the findings, by the Voter Research and Surveys (VRS) consortium, suggested that while the figures may be understated or overstated, the possibility of overstatement could not be ruled out since homosexuals are "more likely to vote; they are more likely to fill out an exit poll questionnaire...."[8]

Dr. J. Gordon Muir reported on a variety of studies in an Op Ed piece in the *Wall Street Journal*—a study in France (1.4% of men and 0.4% of women were found to have had homosexual intercourse in the five years preceding the survey), as well as studies in Britain and at the University of Chicago.[9] Dr. Muir is the author of "Kinsey, Sex and Fraud," (Huntington House Publishers, 1990). Muir points out that:

Although Kinsey had been criticized early on by other scientists, including psychologist Abraham Maslow (whose advice he ignored), the ten percent fallacy was revealed in the mid-

1980s when statisticians began tracking AIDS cases.
Adopting the ten percent estimate then known rates of infection with HIV among gay men, New York City's Department
of Health grossly overestimated the size of the city's HIV
infected gay population as 250,000 (indirectly placing the
total number of homosexual/bisexual men at 400,000 to
500,000). In 1988, these figures had to be revised down to
50,000 and 100,000, respectively. The Centers for Disease
Control has also stopped using the Kinsey data for national
projection.

It was no accident that the ten percent figure became engraved
in stone. In a 1989 book, "After the Ball," a blue print for gay
political activism, Marshall Kirk and Hunter Mattson boast
that "when straights are asked by pollsters for a formal estimate, the figure played back most often is the ten percent gay
statistic which our propagandists have been drilling into their
heads for years."[10]

Use of the ten percent number is intellectually dishonest.

The attempt to enlist ten to fifteen percent of the population as
practicing homosexuals has thus been a propaganda success but is now
becoming a credibility failure. It's one of those things people know
"just ain't so." The ten percent number is now so disproved that making the claim has become intellectually dishonest.

a.   The Kinsey Report, on which the number was based, has been
     shown to be fraudulent.

b.   Recent studies have all honed in on a number between one
     and two per cent for practicing homosexuals.

c.   Homosexuals claim their opponents don't get their facts right.
     Meanwhile, one of the main building blocks of their claims
     for the past two decades was off by 500 percent.

d.   It is now clear that the extent of HIV infection was grossly
     overstated in the mid-1980s because the Center for Disease

Control made the ten percent assumption and multiplied accordingly. In 1980, when we were told that the epidemic was mushrooming, at the same time we were being told it was "now" at 1,500,000 cases. The CDC elected not to admit the error, so as not to infuriate homosexual activists, but merely let the numbers catch up, a sign of the clout of this allegedly oppressed community.

LeGard Smith sums up the evidence well:

In Britain (where private acts of sodomy are exempted from criminal penalty) it is well-publicized that the French believe all Englishmen are "puffs," as homosexuals are called. However, the most recent survey shows that the English are only slightly ahead of the French in that department. In 1987 the British Market Research Bureau carried out a detailed survey for the Department of Health and Social Services' "AIDS" unit. The survey found that only 1.5 percent of males could be described as active homosexuals. (The figures for bisexuals was 1 percent.)[11]

Back home in America, Judith Reisman, author of *Kinsey, Sex and Fraud,* also puts the figure at 1 percent, while Paul Cameron's Washington-based Family Research Institute figure is closer to 3 percent. Connected as they are with more conservative leanings, these figures could be attacked as biased. But they correspond (even generously, in the instance of FRI) with the figures just previously cited, and with what may be the most objective survey taken to date in the United States.[12]

For over 20 years the National Opinion Research Center, a polling group affiliated with the University of Chicago, has conducted the General Social Survey, related to a variety of social issues. NORC's director, Tom W. Smith, reports that between 1989 and 1992 two questions were added to its annual survey, which asked about sexual behavior.

The results have been consistent: Among men, 2.8 percent reported exclusively homosexual activity in the preceding year; among women, 2.5 percent. NORC is still tabulating the results of a full-scale, 3,000-person sexual behavior study, but experts don't expect the numbers to be appreciatively different.[13]

As this book went to press, the latest figures emerged from the National Survey of Men, conducted by the Battelle Human Affairs Research Center in Seattle. Dr. John Billy reports that the 1993 survey revealed that 2.3 percent of all males had had "some homosexual contact" in the past ten years, but that only 1.1 percent had been exclusively homosexual in the previous year.[14] What we are seeing, then, both home and abroad, is that the number of practicing homosexuals is ranging between 1 and 3 percent of the general population—nowhere near the mythical 10 percent. Even the gays are beginning to acknowledge this fact.

And why not? The 10-percent gay propaganda has served its purpose well. Now that the gays have political clout and have helped put their own man in the White House, there's no longer much need to play the deceptive numbers game.[15]

3b. "You may not appreciate this, but gay people have a long and illustrious history. Alexander the Great, Jonathan and David, Plato, Michelangelo, and a host of others have made major contributions to society."

Seeking posthumous endorsement of the homosexual lifestyle on often shaky, and sometimes utterly non-existent evidence, is neither fair to the dead nor relevant to the current issue.

The efforts to enlist endorsements of the homosexual lifestyle from the lips of the dead is both good advertising technique and good tactics. It is hard to disprove. The homosexual activists will, of course, leap on any suspicious reference to infer secret homosexuality. Michelangelo, Da Vinci, Alexander the Great, David and Jonathan (did they not have a "love surpassing the love of women"?), and Tchaikovsky will all give testimony through the mouths of current publicists. While some undoubtedly were homosexual, others undoubtedly were not. And as for many, the evidence may be weak or ambiguous—such as the word of an archenemy or an unmarried status.

It is true that some cultures institutionalized homosexual relations between mature men and adolescent boys. One such society was Sparta.[16] Islam, despite the teaching of the Koran, which formally condemns the practice, has also been associated with significant homosexuality:

> The sexual relations of a mature man with a subordinate youth were so readily accepted in upper-class circles that there was often little or no effort to conceal their existence.[17]

Egyptian culture thought that: "homosexual intercourse with a god was auspicious."[18] These examples do not show that homosexuality is somehow natural, but that where society approves of homosexuality, it tends to increase with all of its ancillary problems.

That some talented people have a deviant lifestyle proves nothing about the value of that lifestyle.

The Judeo-Christian heritage has been characterized by its exaltation of the family and heterosexual monogamy. Not everyone has lived up to these ideals. But what does this prove:

a. The willingness to posthumously implicate worthies of past eras into the homosexual movement often reflects confusion about a variety of attitudes in those eras. It is clear, for example, that Plato idealized relationships among men. Indeed, he used the term "eros" to describe his relationship with his philosophy. But as one professor of classics points out:

Plato rejects homosexual intercourse because it can render men unfit for marriage and because it is contrary to nature and a shameless indulgence. The "Laws" recommends that homosexuality, like adultery, fornication, and the use of prostitutes, not be engaged in; that if it is engaged in, it be kept private or closeted, and that if it is discovered, it be punished by deprivation of civil rights, a severe penalty. In effect, the Laws recommends criminalization.[19]

b. Suppose a number of talented people were homosexual. Is that an endorsement of their sexual propensities? Far more artists and poets have had lives shortened by alcohol or drugs. Does their propensity to engage in self-destructive behavior in any way validate that behavior? In Paul Johnson's *The Intellectuals,* he documents serious character flaws in many heroes of the liberal intelligentsia, people like Bertrand Russell—a liar and cad in his treatment of women; and Rousseau—who impregnated women and abandoned his offspring without an apparent thought of personal responsibility to woman or child; and Lillian Hellman—who he writes about in a chapter called, "Lies, Damn Lies and Lillian Hellman." Does the talent or enduring work of these people in philosophy, the theater, or mathematics, suggest that their personal lifestyle is good and valid? Should one credit the personal demons that dominated these intellectuals with any of their accomplishments? If we like the poetry of Coleridge, does that mean we should go easier on cocaine use?

c. The enlistment of entire societies, like ancient Sparta, is also ineffective as support for homosexual lifestyles. Certain societies did legitimize sodomy between same-sex partners. Egypt memorialized such things on tombs. It was, apparently, fashionable in Canaan and among the Greeks. What such historical illustrations suggest is that homosexual behavior is not genetically determined. Is one to suppose that genes explain why homosexual acts became dominant in certain societies? Were all of these Spartans mutants with a distended hypothalamus? Quite the contrary, *the existence of such widespread sexual deviance shows that the principal influence underlying widespread homosexual behavior is social acceptance of it.* When such sexual behavior is legitimized rather than stigmatized, more people do it. If this is so, the dangers of the gay rights movement is clear. If it succeeds in its goal of making society more accepting of sodomy, it will inevitably lead to more people choosing to experiment with it, and experiencing its destructiveness.

d.   When claiming past societies, one must take the bitter with the sweet. Those societies that have accepted homosexuality, for example, have typically denigrated women. As Dennis Prager points out:

> There appears to be a direct correlation between the prevalence of male homosexuality and the relegation of women to a low societal role. At the same time, the emancipation of women has been a function of Western civilization, the civilization least tolerant of homosexuality.[20]

As another author put it, Athens at the height of its philosophical and artistic greatness was a society dominated by men who sequestered their wives and daughters, denigrated the female role in reproduction, erected monuments to the male genitalia, and had sex with the sons of their peers.[21]

e.   That many people have tried sodomy does not mean it is "natural." That many gifted people have tried it does not make it "natural." It is natural like incest, drunkenness, adultery, egotism, lying, greed, or rape is natural: people feel strong drives to do it and, if not resisted, these drives ripen into habits and ultimately into a lifestyle.

3c. "There are far more of us than you realize. We are all around you. We are your fathers, mothers, brothers and sisters, sons and daughters."

The fact that one may have loved ones involved in a destructive lifestyle ought to make one more alarmed about social acceptance of that lifestyle.

Surely we want to keep those close to us from danger:

- If you were the father of a young man considering a homosexual lifestyle, would you seek to dissuade him? If you knew he was considering a "calling" whose practitioners have an average life expectancy of under fifty years and disproportionate vulnerability to dozens of diseases, would you accept it, or seek to change it?[22]

- We now know that anal sodomy is one of the most dangerous behaviors in America. It is the most efficient route of transmission for the most lethal disease of the century. It is associated with dozens of serious public health problems. Yet there are continuing efforts in state legislatures to remove prohibitions against it. The worse we know it to be, apparently, the less we want to prohibit it.

Promotion of a destructive lifestyle leads to perverse social policy.

- The Department of Health and Human Services issued a report in August 1989 that detailed the enormous rates of suicide among adolescents who experiment with or engage in homosexual behavior.[23] The findings are no surprise to those familiar with the effects of a homosexual lifestyle.

  Analysts both inside and outside the church have viewed homosexuality as a self-destructive lifestyle, yet where does the report place the blame for the phenomenon? If homosexual behavior is *the* variable associated with increased risk of suicide, would it be the behavior itself that is at fault? No, the report counsels. It is the fault of those who advance traditional morality, especially the churches. By calling "bad" something that is "good," they create a climate for teen suicide. If churches stopped teaching the biblical view that homosexuality is a self-destructive lifestyle, homosexuality would stop being a self-destructive lifestyle.

- Syphilis and AIDS have much in common. Both are sexually transmitted. Both are stigmatizing. Both are lethal, if they run their course. But syphilis is generally curable, so it is even more important to stop the transmission of AIDS. Yet California had a law that made it illegal for a doctor (a) not to report a case of syphilis to the Commission of Health and (b) to report a case of AIDS to the same commissioner.[24] He could go to jail if he reported the *more* serious public health problem, or if he did not report the *less* serious one.

These perverse results will continue to multiply as long as proponents of a homosexual agenda are allowed to play the game on their grounds. To win lasting victories, they must keep the focus of public attention on slogans and off facts. Gay rights proponents seek to maintain a high level of abstraction in the debate out of necessity. Once the facts emerge, proponents retreat, like Bunyan's Giant Despair at the first hint of daylight.

3d. "We have the support of most of the religious leadership in our campaign."

Enlisting politically sensitive religious leaders into the gay rights movement is a long-time gay rights objective.

Homosexual militants have long perceived a daunting barrier to their objectives: traditional religious convictions that homosexual behavior is immoral. Just as the homosexual felt stigmatized when his sexual behavior was listed as a "mental disorder" by the psychiatric community, so he feels he cannot be accepted while there remain churches and individuals who believe his conduct is sinful. As a result, homosexuals have not overlooked the battlefield of theology in their campaign for legitimacy.

Homosexuals recognize the political dimensions of theological controversies. If "guerrilla theater" and propaganda can influence scientists to repeal their findings, cannot the same tactics dilute accepted doctrine or engender new church teaching?

To that end, homosexuals began to demand that they be represented in any study done by church officers. The Roman Catholic homosexual group Dignity, for example, demanded of Baltimore's archbishop, William Borders, that the "gay and lesbian" community advise the archbishop on homosexuality.[25] They have sought systematically to make sure opposing voices within the church are not heard. A "gay activist alliance" convinced WOR TV to edit out allegedly anti-homosexual remarks made by evangelist James Robison on his weekly radio program.[26] They have applied substantial pressure on individual church bodies to alter their stance.[27] The reason for the pressure is not difficult to discern.

> There is no question that the main stumbling block in the theoretical and practical acceptance of homosexuality by American society has been traditional religion. This has been perfectly understood by the leadership of the homosexual movement.[28]

Religious leaders have proved especially vulnerable to this homosexual pressure. As David Briggs points out in his lead paragraph reporting on the findings of the Lutheran Commission on Sexuality:

> Masturbation is healthy, the Bible supports homosexual unions, and teaching teens how to use condoms to prevent disease is a moral imperative, says a task force leading the nation's largest Lutheran body into the sex wars.
>
> Four years in the making, a draft statement going before the Evangelical Lutheran Church in America declares that the

core of human sexuality should be loving, committed relationships and not limited to heterosexual marriages.[29]

Religious leaders who endorse homosexuality are out of touch with their constituents.

The denominational committees who offer up such favorable opinions on the "God-given" nature of homosexual orientation are not only contradicting the Bible and traditional teaching of their church; they are almost always well out of line with their own laity, and often with their own rank and file pastors.

A good example is the special Presbyterian Assembly which recommended:

- That "all persons, whether heterosexual or homosexual, whether single or partnered, have a moral right to experience a justice-love in their lives and to be sexual persons."
- That gays and lesbians be received as full participant members, and for ordination, "regardless of their sexual orientation."
- That worship resources be designed to celebrate same-sex relationships.
- That the problem before the church is not sexual sin but the "prevailing social, cultural, and ecclesial arrangements... [and] conformity to the unjust norm of compulsory heterosexuality."

Ultimately, these recommendations came up before the broader constituency. When the recommendation was voted on by the General Assembly, the special assembly was shown to be out of touch. It was voted down 534 to 31. In a pastoral letter, it was said:

This lustful act of homosexuality is denounced but it is not singled out for special attention.[30]

The reason for this disparity is apparent. Gay rights activists work behind the scenes with political elites.

*Religious leaders who endorse homosexuality are out of the main-
stream of traditional moral teaching.*

It is the homosexual militants who are outside the mainstream.
The traditional moral view has an ancient and diverse following. In
538, Emperor Justinian said:

> Since certain men, seized by diabolical incitement, practice
> among themselves the most disgraceful lusts, and act contrary
> to nature: we enjoin them to take to heart the fear of God and
> the judgment to come, and to abstain from such like diabolical
> and unlawful lusts, so that they may not be visited by the just
> wrath of God on account of these impious acts, with the result
> that cities perish with all their inhabitants.[31]

Henry VIII removed cases of sodomy from the ecclesiastical
courts and made them a capital crime, which he called "the detestable
and abominable vice of buggery."[32] Sir Edward Coke wrote: "Buggery
is a detestable and abominable sin, amongst Christians not to be
named, committed by carnal knowledge against the ordinance of the
creator and order of nature."[33] The great legal commentator Blackstone
called homosexuality an act "the very mention of which is a disgrace
to human nature."[34] Many polls have established that religious people
view homosexuality as a sin, and that those who view it as a sin also
overwhelmingly view it as abnormal.

Some approach the matter with humor. Evelyn Waugh once said
when asked why there are no good proofreaders left in England:
"Because clergymen are no longer unfrocked for sodomy."[35]

The homosexual thrust to co-opt religion is complicated by major
religious traditions that acknowledge an authoritative standard. To
some, as in the Roman Catholic tradition, that authority comes from
the official pronouncements of the church, combining the Bible with
church tradition, papal encyclicals, and the like. To others in the
Reformed and Protestant traditions, it comes from the Bible itself. For
both Roman Catholics and Evangelicals, homosexuality traditionally
has been viewed as a grave evil.

But here too homosexuals have made inroads. For these churches, the homosexuals needed to take the religious tradition as a given, but reinterpret it to permit homosexual behavior. At a practical level, homosexuals have sought to penetrate these churches to make their suggested changes in theology more palatable.

Homosexuals use political pressure and confrontation tactics to win religious endorsements.

To win religious endorsements, homosexuals have resorted to the strategy of political pressure and confrontation. First came confrontation. At a major Roman Catholic conference, a "gay liberation front" group interrupted the proceedings to say:

> We are homosexuals!
>
> As members of the Gay Liberation Front, we deny your right to conduct this seminar.
>
> It is precisely such institutions as the Catholic church and psychiatry which have created and perpetuated the immorality myth and stereotype of homosexuality which we as homosexuals have internalized, and from which we now intend to liberate ourselves.[36]

Along with these more confrontational approaches, there have been cooperative endeavors. The homosexual group Dignity sought out sympathetic priests to open churches for fund-raisers, workshops, and various homosexual events. Such approaches sought the sympathy of the Roman Catholic church for homosexuals who wanted to remain in the church even while continuing their conduct. Gradually, the position of many priests and intellectuals in the church began to erode. What used to be a clear case of serious moral disorder became more confusing. Today, many of these churches actually fund homosexual causes. Finally, a prominent Jesuit magazine, *America*, could write:

> The use of biblical injunctions against homosexuality by

Anita Bryant and her followers was hopelessly fundamentalistic. Theological scholarship, whether scriptural or ethical, recognizes today that the application of scripture texts that condemn homosexuality is dubious at best. The phenomenon of homosexuality, as it is understood today, covers too wide a range of inclinations and behavior patterns to be subject to sweeping condemnations. Furthermore, the overall tone and principle argument of the "save our children" campaign not only lack[ed] Christian compassion toward homosexuals but also violated basic justice in perpetuating a lie.[37]

Other Roman Catholics, such as Charles Curran, began to accept the notion that homosexuals could not help themselves, saying, "Some people, through no fault of their own, are homosexual."[38] One Roman Catholic priest has carefully documented the overwhelming infiltration of the Roman Catholic church by the "homosexual network."[39]

The movement has also sought to influence those who look exclusively to the Bible for authority, an endeavor every bit as daunting as infiltration of the Roman Catholic church. But soon there began to appear books such as Ralph Blair's *An Evangelical Look at Homosexuality* and Scanzoni and Mollenkott's *Is the Homosexual My Neighbor? Another Christian View*. Suddenly, what had been clear for centuries was now becoming hazy.

But historic doctrines are stubborn. They stand as a silent witness. Christianity is not alone in its assessment. Every major religious tradition views homosexuality as an inarguable moral offense against a God who created human beings male and female and told them to "fill the earth." Most, if not all, primitive tribes have a taboo against homosexual behavior, reflecting what Paul says in his analysis of homosexuality in Romans 1: God's truth is perfectly plain in nature so that men are without excuse. Even if that plainness escapes the learned divine, it often is clear to the person in the pew.

3e. "Psychologists now recognize that we are not 'sick' or 'mentally ill.' Compelled by scientific evidence, they took homosexuality off a list of mental disorders in the early 70s."

This change in position has nothing to do with new scholarship of any kind. It came about because of political pressure.

That the removal occurred is undisputed. That it had anything to do with science is uninformed. The decision tells more about homosexual tactics than homosexual "normality." A look at how this was brought about again reveals homosexual tactics.

Irving Bieber was a distinguished scholar and primary author of a 1962 book titled *Homosexuality*. One of the foremost psychoanalysts of this century, Bieber had long known that "all psychoanalytic theories assume that homosexuality is psychopathologic."[40]

It was now May 1970 and Bieber had been invited to address the annual meeting of the American Psychiatric Association. Bieber was to appear on a panel addressing the issues of homosexuality and the transsexual. Bieber was of course familiar with the robust debate that characterized serious psychoanalytic discussion. But he was not ready for the kind of tactics that would be used against him on this occasion.

A loosely organized confederation of homosexuals and feminists were preparing to confront him in a way that reflected disdain for the traditional rules of language and logic in Bieber's scholarly profession. Influenced by the radicalization of American politics in 1970, a year that saw the high-water mark of protest, they decided to welcome him with tactics that observers would call "guerrilla theater."[41] As Bieber began to speak, he was immediately the object of shouted taunts from the audience. His voice was drowned out by chants. When he attempted to explain his position, the militants laughed in derision. For Bieber that day there would be no civility, only expressions of rage, name-calling, and vicious personal attack. No wonder one observer described Bieber as in "considerable distress."[42]

In a later session on sexuality, the "guerrillas" again came out in force. A young Australian doctor who had successfully used conditioning techniques in the treatment of perverse sexual practices attempted to read his paper. The visitors in the scholarly audience were not prepared to listen. "Where did you take your residency—Auschwitz?" After using words such as "vicious" and "torture," the demonstrators demanded to take the microphone. The result was pandemonium. Homosexual militants shouted out their outrage and described psychiatry as an instrument of oppression.[43]

Bieber had seen only the vanguard of the homosexual shock troops. Disruptions continued. At the frequently somnolent Convocation of Fellows of the A.P.A., homosexual activists stormed the meeting, grabbed the microphone, and denounced the psychiatrists, seeking to intimidate them from even discussing homosexuality. As one homosexual leader declared, "Psychiatry is the enemy incarnate. Psychiatry has waged a relentless war of extermination against us. You may take this as a declaration of war against you." Some of the psychiatrists viewed the homosexual militants as nothing more than "Nazi storm troopers." The psychiatric profession had never before seen forged credentials, physical intimidation, and brutal rhetoric used at a scholarly meeting.[44]

The object of the homosexuals' fury was, of course, a long-held tenet of the psychiatric profession: Homosexuality, based on a wealth of evidence, is a pathological condition, not a normal outlet of sexual expression. Homosexuality had long been listed in the *Diagnostic and Statistical Manual, Mental Disorders (DSM-I)*. It was, therefore, a "mental disorder." As Dr. Karl Menninger had written several years earlier, "Whatever it be called by the public, there is no question in the minds of psychiatrists regarding the abnormality of such behavior."[45]

Leading psychiatrists have spoken of the decision as a disgrace.

It would have been difficult for Bieber to believe that such brutal, unsophisticated, and unscholarly assaults could change the results of scholarly research. But the homosexual objective was clear. They wanted homosexuality deleted from *DSM-II*. And, shockingly, the homosexual militants won. In what some viewed as a "craven capitulation to the power of the mob,"[46] the A.P.A. decided to delete homosexuality from its list of mental disorders.

Many dissenters were outraged. The profession had "disgraced itself." Another observer said, "It now seems that if groups of people march and raise enough hell, they can change anything in time.... Will schizophrenia be next?"[47] And one psychiatrist wrote: "The board of trustees has made a terrible, almost unforgivable decision which will adversely affect the lives of young homosexuals who are desperately seeking direction and cure. That decision...will give [them] an easy way out."[48] Among the most sensible voices was senior psychiatrist Abram Kardiner who wrote:

> Those who reinforce the disintegrative elements in our society will get no thanks from future generations. The family becomes the ultimate victim of homosexuality, a result which any society can tolerate only within certain limits.
>
> If the American Psychiatric Association endorses one of the symptoms of social distress as a normal phenomenon, it demonstrates to the public its ignorance...and thereby acquires a responsibility for aggravating the already-existing chaos.[49]

Private surveys reveal that most traditional psychiatrists continue to believe that homosexuality is pathological.

A new rhetoric had won the day. But had it really changed the minds of psychiatrists? A revealing, confidential poll later showed that the earlier decision was the product of intimidation. A poll in the journal *Medical Aspects of Human Sexuality*, taken three years after the A.P.A.'s 1974 referendum, sought the views of ten thousand psychiatrists on whether homosexuality was pathological. One analysis of the first responses to the poll revealed that sixty-nine percent continued to believe that homosexuality "usually represented a pathological adaptation." Only eighteen percent disagreed with this proposition. When asked the source of homosexual problems, seventy percent said it was the result of "personal conflicts" rather than social stigmatization.[50]

Bayer sums up what happened to Irving Bieber when confronting homosexuals in the APA:

> His efforts to explain his position to his challengers were met with derisive laughter. Since the norms of civility were considered mere conventions designed to mute outrage, it was not difficult for a protester to call him a Nazi. "I've read your book, Dr. Bieber, and if that book talked about black people the way it talks about homosexuals, you'd be drawn and quartered and you'd deserve it." This verbal attack with its violent tone caused Bieber considerable distress.[51] A tainted victory won by a savage use of verbal weapons became a chief arguing point for homosexuals. Homosexuals now could use the edict of a major academic organization to declare their normalcy.

3f. "We are as normal as 'straight' people."

Experts point out that homosexuality is not normal.

Homosexuals do not simply discover an alternative, perfectly normal form of sexual behavior somehow natural to them. They acquire, through a variety of decisions, influences, and choices, a vulnerability toward, and later a pattern of, behavior that is disordered and dangerous. Dr. Armand Nicholai, chief psychiatrist of the Medical School at Harvard University and editor of *The Harvard Guide to Psychiatry*, said:

> I have treated hundreds of homosexuals. None of them, deep down, thought he was normal. Simulating eating is not eating. Simulating being female is not being female. Simulating sex is not sex.[52]

As another prominent psychiatrist put it:

> Those who urge the acceptance of homosexuality as simply a
> normal form of sexuality, rather than a behavioral disorder,
> developmental arrest or failure, or a clinical illness, reflect the
> blurred boundaries of social behavior which currently impair
> communal health in many ways.[53]

The reason why homosexuals claim their behavior is normal is
apparent. If homosexuality is natural, doing homosexual acts becomes
an accepted solution to relieve pent-up "natural" drives. This solution,
however, creates myriad problems and solves nothing.

As Dr. Socarides, an eminent expert on homosexuality, puts it:

> The "solution" of homosexuality is always doomed to failure
> and, even when used for utilitarian purposes—for example,
> financial benefits when being supported by a partner—is char-
> acterized by strife and turmoil. Homosexuality is...filled with
> destruction and self-deceit. It is a masquerade of life in which
> certain psychic energies are neutralized and held in a
> marginally quiescent state. However, the unconscious mani-
> festations of hate, destructiveness, incest, and fear always
> threaten to break through. Instead of union, cooperation,
> solace, stimulation, emotional enrichment, and a maximum
> opportunity for creative interpersonal maturation and realistic
> fulfillment, there are multiple underlying factors which con-
> stantly threaten any ongoing homosexual relationship:
> destruction, mutual defeat, exploitation of the partner and the
> self, oral-sadistic incorporation, aggressive onslaughts, and
> attempts to alleviate anxiety—all comprising a pseudo-solu-
> tion to the aggressive and libidinal conflicts that dominate and
> torment the individuals involved.[54]

*Accepting homosexuals as "normal" victimizes homosexuals them-
selves.*

The damage to homosexuals goes far beyond their medical problems. Their conduct leads to devastating psychological consequences. Though homosexuals frequently point to the American Psychiatric Association's decision to drop the designation of homosexuality as a sexual deviation (an action that we saw earlier was accomplished through the coercive efforts of homosexual militants), most traditional psychoanalysts continue to believe homosexuality is "a disorder of psychosexual development."[55] The unnatural character of the act and the staggering recent showings of promiscuity have convinced most of the traditionalists that homosexuality is not normal; as one of them characterized it, "homosexuals...present a definite personality maladjustment."[56] According to an influential psychiatrist:

> The homosexual, no matter what his level of adaptation and function in other areas of life, is severely handicapped in the most vital area, namely that of his interpersonal relationships. The homosexual is not only afraid of women and lost to all meaningful relatedness to them as a group and individually, but he also harbors the deepest aggression against men.[57]

Finding that an "obvious failure of function [means] agony, sorrow, tragedy, fear, guilt of both an unconscious and conscious nature which pervades the homosexual's life," he concludes:

> Those apostles of doom and defeat who would have homosexuality declared "natural and normal" disserve the very cause they claim to espouse. Few physicians and other specialists devoted to the principles of scientific rigor and professional integrity will yield to such propaganda. It is the homosexual who will be victimized by these false "friends." True, it is difficult to know that one is ill, but it is far worse to keep experiencing symptoms and yet be told by supposedly qualified people that "You're all right. There's nothing the matter with you. Relax and enjoy it. It's all society's fault."[58]

CHAPTER 4

THE "ALL GOD'S CHILDREN" CLAIM:

Why Homosexuals Claim that Nature Makes Them Do It (Sometimes), Even Though the Assertion Is Demonstrably False

4a. "No one seriously believes homosexuality is somehow an acquired behavior."

The great majority of experts believe homosexuality is an acquired behavior.

This argument is upside down. Few people believe homosexuality is genetically determined. Most believe it is an acquired behavior. Among those who state that homosexuality is acquired behavior are the following:

Wainwright Churchill in *Homosexual Behavior Among Males:*

> There are no sexual instincts in man...human sexuality is entirely dependent upon learning and conditioning. The individual's pattern of sexual behavior is *acquired* [emphasis in original] in the context of his unique experiences and [is] in no sense innate or inherited.[1]

Robert Frumkin in *The Encyclopedia of Sexual Behavior:*

> Without [emphasis in original] specific sexual experiences, man outside of cultures—that is, so-called feral or natural man—or the extreme social isolate, does not generally engage in sexual behavior upon reaching puberty. There is no sexual instinct in man.[2]

H.C. Resnik and Marvin Wolfgang, in *Sexual Behaviors: Social, Clinical, and Legal Aspects:*

One is normally born with a given sex and the capacity to manifest the sex drive, but the expression of that drive is more intimately related to one's culture and social system than any other drive.[3]

William H. Masters, Virginia E. Brown, and Robert C. Kolodny (i.e., Masters and Johnson) in *Human Sexuality:*

The genetic theory of homosexuality has been generally discarded today.... Despite the interest in possible hormone mechanisms in the origin of homosexuality, no serious scientist today suggests that a simple cause-effect relationship applies.[4]

Dr. Charles Socarides in *Homosexuality:*

There is no connection between sexual instinct and the choice of sexual object. Such an object choice is learned, acquired behavior: there is no inevitable genetically inborn propensity towards the choice of a partner of either the same or opposite sex.[5]

Some psychiatrists are more blunt. The famous sexologist Dr. Albert Ellis wrote:

Although I once believed that homosexuals are seriously neurotic, considerable experience with treating many of them (and in being friendly with a number whom I have not seen for psychotherapy) has convinced me that I was wrong! Most fixed homosexuals, I now am convinced, are borderline psychotic or outright psychotic. In every case I have seen, irrational fear played the leading role in inducing the individual to become homosexual in the first place or inducing him to maintain his early acquired homophilic conditioning in the second place.[6]

Edmund Burglar commented on the danger of glamorizing self-destructive behavior:

> The only effective way of fighting and counteracting homosexuality would be the wide dissemination of the knowledge that there is nothing glamorous about suffering from the disease known as homosexuality, that the disease can be cured, and that this apparently sexual disorder is invariably coupled with severe unconscious self-damage that will inevitably show up outside the sexual sphere as well, because it embraces the entire personality.[7]

4b. "Biology now has confirmed that being gay is genetically determined. It is no longer open to serious question."

There is no significant evidence that homosexuality is biologically determined.

The media regularly report on new "discoveries" purported to hint at a genetic link to homosexual behavior. The reports are often promoted uncritically, without review of the substantial evidence that homosexuality cannot be genetically determined. These stories routinely lack careful analysis of the "discovery" and rarely evaluate the authors, often homosexuals themselves, with an obvious agenda.

An overwhelming number of experts have concluded that homosexuality is not principally—or significantly—a genetically induced phenomenon. Many experts are unequivocal on this subject. The eminent William Byne reported in *Archives of General Psychiatry,* March 1993, "There is *no evidence* at present to substantiate a biologic theory" of sexual orientation (emphasis added).[8]

There is substantial evidence that homosexual behavior is not genetic.

There are many phenomena a biologic theory could not explain:

a. Why are at least half of those who have a homosexual twin not homosexual themselves? If genetics determined orientation, why wouldn't all identical twins have the same orientation? If environment determined orientation, why wouldn't twins growing up in an essentially equivalent environment have the same orientation?

b. Why do so many people change their orientation if it is biologically determined? Observers have noted migration into and out of sexual expressions. Women introduced to "swinging," for example, later sometimes report themselves to be bisexual, even though not attracted to same-sex partnerships before that time.

c. There is significant evidence of a relationship between social acceptance of homosexuality and its frequency in a society. (And if so, wouldn't we rationally try to discourage the marginal person from becoming involved with it, given its short life expectancies, associated diseases, alarming rates of suicide and alcoholism, and its costs to the public?) As some past societies had widespread homosexuality—Sparta, for example, or ancient Egypt—what does that say about a common biological cause?

Although gay rights laws often speak of "affectional preference," and homosexuals speak of the joys of "gay liberation," homosexuals on the defensive frequently say they have no choice. They are imprisoned by nature. Responsibility for sexual practices is shuffled to one side by claims they are born that way, or merely discover and affirm what they are naturally; and they cannot change their nature. On such points, the factual evidence is increasingly clear.

Although an occasional study may hint at some biological reason for homosexuality, nearly all modern analysts support the conclusion that homosexuals are not born that way. They learn to be that way:

> The question is often asked if there is not some kind of genetic or hormonal factor, innate or inborn, which accounts

for this condition. Homosexuality, the choice of a partner of the same sex for orgastic satisfaction, is not innate.[9]

A famous radio personality, exposed for homosexual activity, purportedly said he could not help it because it "is in my genes." Modern medicine has confirmed that this is not the case. As Dr. James McCary, author of *Sexual Myths and Fallacies*, points out: "Neither present day endocrinological tests nor microscopic or clinical examinations have revealed any physiological differences between the heterosexual and homosexual individual."[10]

The *British Journal of Psychiatry* reviewed evidence from the study of forty-six sets of identical and fraternal twins which showed that only twenty percent of the siblings of homosexuals were homosexuals themselves. The conclusion was that genetics were "insufficient" explanation for homosexual behavior.[11]

One study of the hypothalamus (a small appendage at the base of the brain), revealed that the size of the hypothalamus was larger in homosexual males than in heterosexual males. The finding caused quite a stir in the media. Putting aside the homosexual interests of the author, the effect of AIDS on the brain, the variations within heterosexuals, homosexuals who have given up the practice, and the utter absence of such data for lesbian women, what is one to say about societies that have widespread anal sodomy? Was there something in the water that expanded the Spartan hypothalamus? Even homosexual writers have seen the defects in the argument.[12]

4c. "Some people are right-handed and some people are left-handed. Some are gay and some are straight. No one chooses his or her sexual orientation. No one can change it."

Change is possible for a homosexual who has a sincere desire to do so.

Whether homosexuals can change their orientation is, for some, a key argument in the gay rights debate. That, of course, is not the only issue. Even if homosexual orientation were unchangeable, that would not mean that homosexual activity must continue. But if homosexuals cannot change their orientation, it makes their analogy to other civil rights groups more compelling.

Some early psychiatric opinion suggested that change in sexual orientation was rarely feasible. Recent studies have shown, however, that homosexuality need not be a permanent condition. Homosexuals *can* change.[13] The key is whether they want to.

The purported unchangeableness of the homosexual is belied by findings of traditional psychotherapists. Irving Bieber's study of seventy-two patients revealed that thirty-eight percent had become heterosexuals or bisexuals and twenty-seven percent had shifted from homosexuality and bisexuality to exclusive heterosexuality.[14] Sex therapists William Masters and Virginia Johnson found, after a fifteen-year study, that they were successful in helping two-thirds of the men and women who indicated a desire to become exclusively heterosexual.[15] One psychiatric survey concludes that "psychotherapy appears to be unsuccessful in only a small number of patients of any age in whom a long habit is combined with...lack of desire to change."[16]

When homosexuality is viewed as a behavior rather than as an identity, it can be changed using basic psychological counseling techniques. Without underestimating the struggle required to break such a deeply ingrained and habitual sexual pattern, the recent evidence of successful transformations into normal sexual patterns is too abundant to ignore. Both Christian organizations and secular psychiatrists have accumulated substantial clinical evidence that the homosexual can change—with adequate support, encouragement, and motivation.[17]

This evidence contradicts the popular lore that "once gay, always gay." Until the 1930s and 1940s, the same pessimism infected popular attitudes about drunkards. They were seen as hopeless derelicts and a burden to society. Now no sensible person doubts that alcoholics can and do recover and gain or regain a useful place in society.

During the past decade a variety of groups, both religious and secular, have emerged to demonstrate the truth of their conviction that homosexuals can change. These groups are making advances into territory not previously explored. Their endurance suggests a hopeful future. Some, like Homosexuals Anonymous, are patterned directly after Alcoholics Anonymous. The best of these groups have one thing in common: they emphasize the importance of personal responsibility for change, learning to make responsible choices with the help of others.

The truly compassionate people are those who are helping homosexuals overcome their condition. Joseph Nicolosi, author of *Reparative Therapy of Male Homosexuality*, is an eminent psychotherapist who, like Socarides and even Masters and Johnson, has had significant success in treating homosexuals. He laments the abdication of his discipline in the face of political and social pressure:

> Psychology and psychiatry have abandoned a whole population of people who feel dissatisfied with homosexuality.[18]

To say "once gay, always gay" is like the old myth of "once a drunk, always a drunk."

What alcoholics learned is that an honest "coming out," without excuses or rationalizations but with a sincere desire to change, is a powerful tool for success. They found that a humble declaration of need evokes not just compassion but respect from others. That same reservoir of good will and helpfulness awaits the humble homosexual who wants to change.

Homosexuals can change. But they need to understand that their behavior is unacceptable. Just as it would be ludicrous to call for alcoholics rights or to have a day celebrating drunkenness, it is equally ludicrous to call for gay rights legislation or to have a day celebrating perversion. The alcoholic discovers in A.A. that the fault is not with others (society, wife, boss) but with himself; likewise the responsibility for change lies not with others, but with himself. Those enablers who accepted him—made up excuses for his absence from work, explained away the bruises he left on children, rationalized his behavior as inherited—were facilitating his collapse. So, too, the public acceptance of homosexuality expressed in gay rights laws and gay pride days provides an easy way out for those who want to appear tolerant and loving, but in actuality it promotes conduct destructive to the homosexual himself.

As one changed homosexual, Anthony Falzarano, reports, "Homosexuality is certainly not innate. It is a learned behavior."[19] Falzarano was one of Roy Cohn's "kept boys" who turned away from homosexuality and is now married with two children.[20]

The old term "sexual preference" is not completely out of line. A four-year study of 124 homosexuals revealed that ninety-two percent of homosexual men had dated a woman at some time, and two-thirds had had sexual intercourse with a woman.[21]

Prager makes the comment:

Whether or not homosexuals choose homosexuality is entirely unrelated to the question of whether society ought to regard it as an equally valid way of life....

Chosen or not, homosexuality remains opposable. If chosen, we argue against the choice; if not chosen, we offer compassion while retaining our heterosexual marital ideals.[22]

4d. "It's terribly unfair to permit discrimination against someone who can't help the way he or she is."

Even if one's sexuality were fixed, that would not be a sufficient reason to grant special legal protection.

Even where the lack of a genetic cause is conceded, some might still argue that homosexual orientation is acquired so early in life that it might as well be genetic. If it is determined by age three or four and permanently fixed, shouldn't it be regarded as involuntary or immutable?

That analysis ignores two things. Even if propensity toward homosexuality is acquired early, that does not distinguish homosexuality from a variety of other tendencies which may afflict people early in life. Psychologists may discern a bent to steal, to be abusive, or to rebel quite early in life. Those inclinations—what religious people might call temptations—if nurtured may develop into hardened behavioral practices. But it would be strange for a thief to claim protected status of the civil rights laws because his inclination to steal began early in life and has now hardened into an immutable lifestyle. Second, there is substantial evidence that homosexuals can change wherever there is a willingness to change.

It is not necessary to act out desires, however strong; many normal people are pure before marriage and faithful after marriage, notwithstanding strong normal desires.

In whatever way the desires become implanted, some homosexuals choose to act on them while others do not. Having a desire is no moral sanction of that desire. Existence does not establish legitimacy. Despite the fact that these desires, when acted upon, are shown to have destructive consequences, homosexual advocates continue to offer ambiguous tests to challenge the overwhelming consensus, based on thorough scientific research, that homosexuality is a learned behavior.

The homosexuals' claim that they have an immutable nature is advanced as an important rationale for the creation of gay rights laws.[23] The key element is choice. If homosexuals cannot help being homosexual, their argument for minority status seems more analogous to other civil rights claims.

Even if immutability could be proved, this alone is not a sufficient reason to give such protections. Many characteristics are immutable but not protected. The Sermon on the Mount asks, "Who of you by worrying can add a single cubit to his height?" Height is, at least without radical surgery, immutable, but height (or lack of it) is not protected. Biology suggests that an additional chromosome may predispose some people to criminal conduct. That formation of chromosomes is immutable, but the class of persons committing sociopathic behavior is not protected. Even without embracing Skinnerian determinism, one can believe that a great number of qualities and dispositions of people are largely immutable: good looks, mannerisms, predisposition to becoming fat.[24] It is clear that immutability is not an adequate reason to grant special status.

Those who advance gay rights measures ignore substantial evidence that homosexual behavior is not innate or immutable. As we point out above, most psychiatrists view the innate or genetic explanation of homosexual behavior as a "myth" or "fallacy."[25] If homosexual behavior is not innate, it is therefore learned or acquired. It is not, as Dr. Socarides points out, "inevitable."

THE ARGUMENT:

*How Doing Sexually Deviant Acts Can Make a
Minority Worthy of Civil Rights Protection*

5a. "We're not asking for anything special. We only want what heterosexual couples have."

It makes perfect sense for public policy to protect and promote the family.

Archimedes said, "Give me a place to stand and I will move the world." The homosexuals need a fulcrum to move the world their way. They find it in the demand for civil rights. By making the majority feel guilty about the prominence given to the family and the unequal social status given to those who reject it, they seek to create momentum to move society toward a value-free sexuality.

Society need not be ashamed of promoting the family. Strong families are the foundation of a strong society. Through providing essential services to society, such as procreation, education, character formation, and protection and provision for young and old, the family renders incalculable benefits that society can reasonably reward.

The U.S. Supreme Court has recognized the centrality of the family. In an opinion on the right of privacy, Justice Harlan said:

> The right of privacy most manifestly is not an absolute. Thus, I would not suggest that adultery, homosexuality, fornication and incest are immune from criminal enquiry, however privately practiced...but the intimacy of husband and wife is necessarily an essential and accepted feature of the institution of marriage, an institution which the State not only must

allow, but which always and in every age it has fostered and protected.[1]

Homosexuality, on the contrary, is essentially anti-family. It encourages promiscuous sexuality, a self-centered morality, and socially irresponsible behavior that exacts huge costs from society. The law has every right to discourage people from entering into paths that are demonstrably destructive—physically and psychologically—first to themselves, then to society itself.

The attempt to construct an analogy between being black or female and committing sodomy is flawed.

Most ordinances giving special protections to homosexuals have been enacted by the false comparison of homosexuality to legally recognized minority groups. By adopting a status word not descriptive of their behavior ("gay"), homosexuals have successfully deflected attention from their conduct. Some statutes still describe homosexual activity as an "abominable and detestable crime against nature." The success activists have had in moving the discussion away from behavior has caused many to accept uncritically their minority status. Some respected judges have found the analogy attractive. Justice Tobriner, writing for the California Supreme Court in *Gay Students Association* v. *Pacific Telephone and Telegraph Co.*, thought it compelling:

> Indeed the subject of the rights of homosexuals incites heated political debate today and the "gay liberation movement" encourages its homosexual members to attempt to convince other members of society that homosexuals should be accorded the same fundamental rights as heterosexuals. The aim of the struggle for homosexual rights, and the tactics employed, bear a close analogy to the continuing struggle for civil rights waged by blacks, women and other minorities.[2]

Some commentators sensitive to civil liberties found the decision full of "stirring language" and "heartening."[3]

Laudatory comments notwithstanding, the analogy between groups defined by race or sex, religious conviction, or national origin and those who practice particular forms of behavior which are, as often as not, criminal,[4] is not self-evident.

Close enough, say homosexuals about the distended analogy. And they have set about to remove obstacles by using the analogy without apology. But to make the analogy work requires covering up the distinctions between racial status and homosexual behavior.

Many states make sodomy a crime, and these statutes have ancient roots. Sodomy was a criminal offense of common law and was forbidden by the laws of all the thirteen original states at the time the Bill of Rights was ratified. Although such statutes are now largely unenforced except in special circumstances (rape, child molestation, or various plea bargain compromises), it is hard to conceive how a group can achieve social acceptance of what they do when society has already decided to make what they do criminal and punishable by imprisonment.

The Supreme Court has ruled that homosexual sodomy, unlike race, has no constitutional protection.

Given this legal dilemma, homosexuals have sought through political or judicial means to have these laws invalidated, and in some states they have succeeded. Those efforts proved ultimately unavailing before the federal courts, however, when the Supreme Court ruled in *Bowers v. Hardwick* that a state law prohibiting consensual sodomy was constitutional.[5]

Homosexuals also sought refuge in a "right to privacy,"[6] the equal protection clause,[7] and various other theories attacking employment discrimination.[8] Since none of these refuges provided much protection, homosexuals adopted the more viable strategy of avoiding that legal thicket altogether. Instead, using to full effect the emotional power of appeals for rights and against discrimination, homosexuals began to propose ordinances that forbid discrimination in housing, employment, and public accommodations based on a person's "affectional or sexual preference" or "affectional or sexual orientation."

Using this strategy, homosexual activists have had a measure of success. Perhaps the most publicized effort was when President Bill Clinton tried to have homosexuals accepted into the military. General Colin Powell put it well in a letter to Representative Patricia Schroeder (D-Colo.):

> Skin color is a benign, non-behavioral characteristic. Sexual orientation is perhaps the most profound of human behavioral characteristics. Comparison of the two is a convenient but invalid argument.[9]

5b. "We are a legitimate minority, just like those who have won similar protections before us."

Civil rights theory is intended to protect true status, not behavior.

The true test of a minority is not one of behavior, but of status. Homosexuals can be characterized by what they do (sodomy) and with whom they do it (their own sex). What gay rights laws ask for is a special privilege for homosexual behavior not generally available to other groups, such as those who commit incest, adultery, bestiality, pedophilia, or, for that matter, any other criminal or antisocial behavior.

In the last two decades, gay rights activists have begun to press a new, radically different set of claims to civil rights protection. Human rights statutes historically have granted special legal standing to those "discrete and insular minorities"[10] who share an immutable *status*. That status was generally unrelated to behavior, traditional perceptions of moral character, or public health. One's racial inheritance, for example, creates a true *status*. Race tells us nothing about a person's lifestyle or behavior. Removing race as a criterion of social decision-making therefore makes sense to all but the most arbitrary decision-maker.

Gay rights proposals redefine status without ever saying so. Rather than acknowledge that such laws protect behavior—say, the act of anal sodomy—whose benefits or detriments to society must be objectively evaluated before the protection is given, proponents create a new minority status. An uncritical acceptance of that new status evades rational inquiry into the underlying behavior and hides the fact that the only cohesive element in this minority is the inclination to commit sodomy with members of the same sex.

This jump from true status to behavior-based status creates the potential for innumerable protected classes ranging from sexual to recreational behaviors, from serious to frivolous interests, from committed involvements to take-it-or-leave-it hobbies. How does one decide, for example, whether to protect classes of such demographic variety as smokers, philatelists, spelunkers, adulterers, bikers, or law review contributors?

This does not mean that no behavior-based status can ever be the subject of special legal privileges or protections. It only suggests that behavior-based status must be analyzed differently—and far more cautiously—than true status. Good public policy demands that sensible judgments be made on the behavior which will be given special status. One must ask the right questions. Is this behavior worthy of special status? What is its impact on society? On those who practice it? Is it morally neutral—at least from the standpoint of conventional and sincerely held moral systems?

The moral force of the civil rights movement has caused many to make this jump uncritically, to treat gay rights as desirable and indistinguishable from the claims made for true status. Two states and approximately fifty other municipalities now prohibit discrimination against homosexuals under general human rights provisions.[11] Certain states prohibit discrimination against homosexuals in more narrow settings, such as public housing. Other states have executive orders that prohibit some forms of discrimination against homosexuals.

Hitching their wagon to the broadly based support Americans

have traditionally given civil rights laws, gay rights advocates have made surprising progress in the past decade.

Adding homosexuals to the list of protected minorities meets none of the traditional requirements for creating special protection.

The human rights analogy, though popular and politically understandable, cannot withstand careful analysis. Adding homosexual behavior to a list of classes that includes racial and religious minorities makes no sense. The tenuous balance of social interests represented by these laws is reflected in the few, and carefully chosen, classes they protect. Relief has been given only in extraordinary circumstances. To acquire protected class status, at least five requirements must be met:

1. A demonstrable pattern of discrimination

2. That is based on criteria that are arbitrary and irrational

3. Causing substantial injury

4. To a class of people with an unchangeable or immutable status

5. Which has no element of moral fault.

Each of these requirements needs to be examined.

1. *A demonstrable pattern of discrimination.* The discrimination alleged must be more than a collection of isolated instances. There must be a clear pattern. At some time or other everyone has been a victim of discrimination. A nervous applicant has lost a job opportunity because someone didn't like his tie or handshake or hairstyle. The beef-eater has been snubbed by the animal-rights militant; the vegetarian has suffered the insults of the red-meat enthusiast. Everyone has an anecdote of some opportunity lost unfairly. The coercive power of law will only intervene, however, where there is a pervasive practice of discrimination throughout society. As was shown in the previous section, however, evidence of such a pattern of discrimination against homosexuals is almost totally lacking.

2. *Based on criteria that are arbitrary and irrational.* Civil rights

laws do not limit anyone's freedom to make rational choices. They simply cancel a license to be prejudiced and to indulge irrational whims.

When it comes to making choices among people, however, deviant sexual behavior tells significantly more about a person's character, or at least his characteristics, than does race, color, or religion. Even when done consensually and in private, homosexual behavior has spill-over effects with public dimensions because it is a self-destructive, disproportionately disease-ridden behavior.[12]

Taking into account a person's perverted sexual orientation is neither arbitrary nor irrational. If the operator of a day-care center knows that a homosexual applicant statistically is a significant health risk, that he is peculiarly susceptible to infections especially dangerous for young children, and that his promiscuity makes him anything but an appropriate role model for the children, is it socially responsible to make it illegal to take such relevant factors into consideration? Already some doctors are calling for more discriminating standards regarding who can give blood or work as food handlers or care for the physically weak—all as a result of shocking discoveries of homosexual health hazards. Is the law prepared to coerce people into ignoring facts that their common sense, moral convictions, and increasing medical knowledge tell them are relevant? If so, there may emerge a disrespect for the very laws in which many deserving minority groups have found refuge.

3. *Causing substantial injury.* Public policy suggests that the creation of far-reaching rights ought not to be done in the absence of extensive wrongs and injuries. A substantial rationale for civil rights protection for blacks was, of course, a century of disproportionate access to wealth and other social benefits. Economists might differ on the reasons for this disproportionate sharing in social benefits, but the fact of disparate social status was clear.

Living with human beings in an imperfect world requires mutual tolerance. Society does not want to encourage people to run to the courts with every complaint, to guard tender egos from every slight, to seek damages for every insult. Laws give protection where the damage is demonstrably substantial. As the arguments of the previous section make clear, no such damage to homosexuals has been demonstrated.

4. *To a class of people with an unchangeable or immutable status.* Perhaps even before the prophet Jeremiah observed that the Ethiopian could not change his color nor a leopard his spots, no one has questioned that everyone has, from the moment of birth, certain unchangeable features. Race, color, and national origin never change. The curious case of transsexuals notwithstanding, the same is true of sex. Each is what the law calls "an immutable characteristic." Although a person's religion may be for some a family inheritance and for others a personal decision, in neither case is it generally considered a whimsical preference. It is—if it means anything worthwhile—a set of deeply rooted, unchanging convictions that to the true believer is as unchangeable as his race, and that he has decided to embrace no matter the cost. At the very least, it is an expression of a long-recognized entitlement to have an opinion and express it. Aside from gay rights laws, no human rights law protects behavior. Certainly none protects preferences.

5. *Which has no element of moral fault.* Human rights laws were never intended to give a social blessing to immorality. The classes they protect are all morally neutral. No moral fault is attached to being black or white, a native or an immigrant, a male or a female. The moral innocence of the victim of discrimination has made the need for such laws compelling. On the other hand, the inveterate liar, the flagrantly unfaithful husband, and the dishonest merchant should not be surprised at the social stigma their behavior produces. If some people prefer not to associate with a compulsive womanizer who constantly boasts of his amorous conquests, it is little wonder that they are not keen to associate with the average homosexual who has ten times as many partners as the most voracious heterosexual. Part of the wisdom of the human rights laws is to focus only on groups that all agree are morally neutral; without such a focus, social support for such legislation could crumble.

Making private judgments based on perceptions of moral character is legitimate and is not "imposing values" on society.

Gay rights laws are occasionally supported by an ideological twist on these facts.[13] Some argue that these laws are necessary to prevent a moral agenda from interfering with our pluralistic society, and that homophobia stands in the way of full equality. Those who advocate conventional morality will necessarily frustrate the legitimate aspirations of a minority whose moral views differ. Homosexuality, by this standard, is simply an "alternative lifestyle" of equal morality and propriety as heterosexual behavior. Recognizing its legitimacy subverts the "establishment" of narrow, sectarian morality.

Such an argument is equally sectarian. One can construct a philosophical system which affirms the morality of all forms of sexual expression, including incest, bestiality, necrophilia, transvestism, or indecently exposing oneself. To a person with this philosophical inclination, it is unfair or unreasonable to discriminate on the basis of which particular form of sexual expression one chooses. But such a relativistic moral scheme is not shared by all. Some might consider homosexual sodomy legitimate under certain circumstances but shrink at bestiality—or believe the converse. A narrow slice of society might see nothing wrong with consensual sexual activity with minors; most abhor it.

Such divisions are to be expected in a pluralistic society and reflect the reason the analogy between homosexual behavior and genetic status breaks down. Character ought to be a relevant criterion. Because it ought to be a relevant criterion, people will assess character differently in a free society. No one can seriously argue that there is moral fault in being black or female, German or Chinese. But as the Supreme Court has recently stated, "To hold that the act of homosexual sodomy is somehow protected as a fundamental right would be to cast aside millennia of moral teaching."[14] To prohibit the use of such a criterion is, therefore, to take away a fundamental right of association, based on a good faith perception of moral character.

In short, gay rights laws meet none of the traditional requirements for human rights protection. Homosexuals have never been able to demonstrate a convincing pattern of discrimination that causes them substantial socioeconomic injury. They are a class of people linked together through behavior, not unchangeable status. Their actions are not morally neutral. Reasonable people—for reasons of deep-seated moral conviction, of health, of psychological stability, or of common sense—may wish to take a person's homosexual lifestyle into account in their decision-making, all without the slightest tinge of bigotry or irrationality.

> **5c. "We have been subject to a pernicious pattern of discrimination. We have been denied basic rights and privileges. We are an underclass."**

Homosexuals are most certainly not an underclass.

Homosexuals are far from an underclass. Average income for male homosexuals was reported to be $42,689 by an "overlooked opinions" survey. The finding for lesbians was $36,072. Both figures were for 1991. The average for the population in general was $30,126.[15] *USA Today* also reported on homosexual affluence: Gay male couples had a $56,863 household income; married couples $47,012; heterosexual unmarried couples, $37,602.[16]

The argument that homosexuals are an underclass is ludicrous. The assumption underlying gay rights laws is, however, to the contrary. It assumes homosexuals need special protections described as "rights." Gays should have basic rights, the argument runs, and some of these rights have been abridged. One may disagree with a person's preferences, after all, without denying him his rights.

Such language begs the question. If homosexuals really have the rights they claim, then they should not be abridged. A right is a moral and legal entitlement. It is the making of a claim that society must rightfully acknowledge. But one fact is often lost in the debate: homosexuals have rights already. Homosexuals have legal rights identical to those of any other citizen. They may exercise their rights to free speech, to assemble, to exercise any religious preference, to be safe in their houses from unreasonable searches, to confront their accusers, to demand a jury trial in a civil or criminal proceeding. They may own property, travel abroad, buy and sell, and enter into enforceable contracts. They are armed with all of the same kinds of rights other Americans cherish.

There is no substantial evidence that demonstrates any significant deprivation for homosexuals. Homosexuals are among the most influential members of modern society.

The legislative history of gay rights ordinances is typically long on emotion and short on evidence. There are no rigorous studies, and no substantial testimony, that prove homosexuals are routinely discriminated against. The legislative history underlying past battles over civil rights was filled with evidence that blacks suffered systematic discrimination against them in the South and structural forms of deprivation, such as isolation, in the North. Disparities in income, housing, employment, cultural opportunities, and education were not merely suspected, they were demonstrated by statistics, sociological studies, and voluminous testimony.

Lack of such proof here is no accident. As one observer has pointed out, "One of the most striking phenomena of the past few years is what appears to be a massive increase in the acceptability of homosexual behavior in America."[17] Aside from social pressure on those flaunting personality traits that would make heterosexuals equally unpopular, people do not routinely discriminate against homosexuals. Homosexuals live in nice neighborhoods, in well-furnished homes and apartments. They are popular in athletics (Billy Jean King, Martina Navratilova), in the arts (Rock Hudson, Boy George, Liberace, Truman Capote, and a long list of others), in Congress

(Congressman Barney Frank), and in the professions.[18]

Indeed, homosexuals have become so strong in the marketplace that nearly every major manufacturer of consumer goods has a marketing plan directed specifically to them. Homosexuals have become a new "power bloc" that has both "votes and money."[19] One writer estimated that homosexuals control one-third of the buying power in California.[20] The estimate is inflated, but there is no doubt about homosexual influence. One wealthy New York homosexual estimated that homosexuals annually control as much as twenty billion dollars in New York City alone.[21] *Blueboy* magazine, a *Playboy*-style publication for homosexuals, found that its readers fit a classically middle-class profile. One homosexual has said that the "dominant style of New York…is set by visible homosexuals."[22]

This is exactly what an economist would anticipate in a free-market economy. When people have to pay a significant price to discriminate, they generally don't discriminate.[23] Homosexuals' influence is seen in their influence with President Clinton. As one observer put it:

> If the gays ever wanted a calling card, they have it in the current President. "Bill Clinton is the Abraham Lincoln of the lesbian and gay community," said Gregory King, a spokesman for the Human Rights Campaign Fund, a pro-gay political group whose 75,000 members raised 2.5 million dollars for the Clinton Campaign.[24]

The homosexual does not need special privileges.

The lack of compelling need for these laws makes clear the true nature of the homosexual agenda.

The homosexuals' failure to demonstrate a need for civil rights protections suggests that the true agenda for their activism is not to rectify a limited list of social grievances based on historic rights. Instead, they want public acknowledgment that the homosexual lifestyle is as valid and upright as that of the heterosexual, and that they are entitled to the same deference as blacks, religious groups, or women. One brochure put out by the Minnesota Committee for Gay and Lesbian Rights talks about the violation of "the most basic right—respect as people."[25]

They want respect and acceptance of their behavior, an acceptance that is good neither for them nor for society.

One prominent psychiatric expert in the treatment of homosexuals is Dr. Charles Socarides, whose textbook on homosexuality is widely used in medical schools and who has written a number of journal articles on the treatment of homosexuals. Dr. Socarides believes that widespread acceptance of homosexuality is the worst thing that could happen to homosexuals since it ignores something the homosexual knows better than anyone else—that his actions are perverted and abnormal and require treatment. This is a terrible injustice for the homosexual, according to Socarides, and impairs our communal health.[26]

Homosexuals already have rights.

In addition to such protections of law shared with all citizens, a homosexual can:

- form organizations to lobby for his political rights
- incorporate under state incorporation law
- form student organizations on state-supported campuses, including rights to the same benefits received by any other campus organizations, such as organized social functions and homosexual dances on campus
- obtain tax-exempt and tax-deductible status
- publicly assemble, rally, petition, and carry out all forms of political activism in support of his political ideas
- wear badges and buttons in public schools and colleges without fear of disciplinary action by the school

•force a public high school principal to allow him to take a male to the school prom as a date

•compel television and radio stations to include members of the homosexual community in determining "community needs"

•be employed under the Civil Service. The Civil Service Commission has given the following directive to its supervisors: "You may not find the person unsuitable for Federal employment merely because that person is a homosexual or has engaged in homosexual acts."

This litany of rights is by no means exhaustive. The homosexual has all the rights the heterosexual does, but he wants a right the heterosexual does not have. He wants to coerce others not to take into account his inclination to practice sodomy, his prevailing preference, even when those others, including parents, employers, or landlords, have contrary convictions. The result expands the privileges given to homosexuals and shrinks the rights of other citizens.

5d. "All the diverse ways people live together should be treated equally by the law. How would you like to be unemployed and homeless simply because others don't approve of your lifestyle?"

Homosexuals are far from an underclass in political influence. The Human Rights campaign fund homosexual political action committee is one of the top ten independent PACs in the nation. It spent well over $1 million in 1987, not even an election year, and had three full-time lobbyists.[27]

5e. "Don't confuse the issue with scare stories about churches. Free expression is protected by the Constitution. Churches are not affected by gay rights laws."

Churches have been and are directly affected by gay rights laws. Gay rights laws have been held to void claims to free expression of religion under the First Amendment.

To appease religious people, promoters of gay rights measures sometimes argue that such measures cannot and will not interfere with religious liberties. Or they advance ambiguous exemptions purporting to limit the effects of such laws. Those who have seen the results of such laws, however, have reason to worry.

Georgetown University is a traditional Roman Catholic school with a strong reputation for academic excellence and a staunch commitment to Roman Catholic moral teaching. Located in Washington, D.C., the university is subject to the laws of the municipality. Among those laws is the District of Columbia Human Rights Ordinance, enacted in 1981, which forbids discrimination in the use of public facilities on the basis of "sexual orientation."[28]

Proponents of the measure, in Washington as elsewhere, had emphasized that it would not be construed to interfere with sincerely held religious views. And so, when the Law Center, the university law school, saw the organization of a "Gay Rights Coalition," the university refused to recognize it or permit it to use university facilities to promote sexual behavior that is immoral and perverted, according to historic Roman Catholic doctrine. The university argued that it was constitutionally entitled to the free exercise of its religious beliefs under the First Amendment and should not be compelled to sacrifice its convictions and violate its conscience by allowing its facilities to be used to affirm unnatural sexuality.

The Gay Rights Coalition sued based on the ordinance. The court thus had to determine which claim had priority: the constitutional right to free exercise of religion or the D.C. Human Rights Act. The court decided that the "compelling government interest" in eliminating discrimination based on sexual orientation outweighed the interference with the university's religious convictions and compelled the university to open its facilities for teachings antithetical to its religious faith.[29]

The result was a clear signal to churches and church-related organizations and institutions, as well as to individuals with religious or moral convictions on homosexuality. When a bona fide religious conviction collides with a gay rights ordinance, the constitutionally protected conviction may give way.

Gay rights laws put sincere religious people in jeopardy.

At approximately the same time, Father Buchanan, a Roman Catholic priest in St. Paul, was interviewing candidates for eighth-grade music teacher at Holy Childhood School. A candidate listed past school employment in music and, based on his resume, seemed qualified. The priest's suspicions were raised, however, when the man insisted he wanted to teach boys. Further research revealed that he was a homosexual. The decision for the priest was easy—his religious convictions and prudence dictated that he not permit a homosexual on the faculty.

Again, the candidate sued, this time under the St. Paul gay rights ordinance which was identical to the one in Minneapolis. The human rights agency made a preliminary determination of discrimination; the file had been turned over to the St. Paul city attorney for criminal prosecution, with possible sanctions including a ninety-day jail sentence and a three hundred dollar fine, when the St. Paul voters overwhelmingly repealed the gay rights ordinance. Like many similar ordinances around the country, the St. Paul ordinance, once put before the voters, lost by a landslide.

5f. "Who is hurt by giving us our rights?"

Adding gay rights to the law has the effect of taking away rights from others.

All rights have corresponding duties. Every newly created right gives rise to a corresponding duty in others. If a homosexual has the right to teach sex education courses in a public school, the school has a duty to allow him to do so, and the parent of a child in that school loses his right to have a say in the moral caliber of a person who teaches his child. If a homosexual has a right to rent a room in a rooming house owned by Mrs. Murphy, Mrs. Murphy loses her right to control the moral caliber of people who live in her house. Compare the following, admittedly fanciful, extremes:

A poor law student approaches Mrs. Murphy's door to see about the twenty-five-dollar-per-week room he had read about in the classified ads. Mrs. Murphy eyes him warily. She asks a series of questions, concluding with, "Do you like the music of J.S. Bach?" "Yes," he answers, somewhat confused. "Then you'll never rent a room from me!" she says and slams the door. What are the student's rights?

Two homosexuals, from an outlandish extreme of the movement, approach Mrs. Murphy's door, one in lipstick and wobbly high heels, the other dressed in leather and jeans, wearing a menacing chain around his neck. They inquire about the room. Mrs. Murphy, annoyed at their appearance and their distasteful, overtly sexual behavior, yells "No, thank you!" through a crack in the door and runs back into her rooming house. What are their "rights"?

Before the passage of a gay rights law, both the student and the homosexuals have the same rights: none. Mrs. Murphy's dislike for Bach may have been opinionated, ignorant, or confused. But the student has no right to claim special protection of the law for any of his personal preferences, whether they be a preference for Bach, cats, or peanut butter. Mrs. Murphy may not like his looks, his children, or his automobile. His only choice is to stop at the next advertised apartment on his want-ads checklist.

Before a gay rights law, situation number two comes out the same way. Here Mrs. Murphy seems on more solid ground. Her decision is based not on a whim but on her perception of the potential tenants' characters. Nonetheless, after passage of such a law, the homosexuals win a privilege for their unnatural sexual practices that the student does not have for his baroque musical tastes, or the average citizen for his normal preferences. The homosexuals can sue...and win.[30]

Laws that protect sexual preferences create a new and privileged class. From all the now-unprotected preferences there are in the world—for clothes, cars, gourmet food, pets, music, poetry—the gay rights laws carve out a special set of preferences related to perverted sexual behavior and give it a special protection available to no one else.[31]

Gay rights laws are coercive to people of conscience.

The controversy boils down to this: Should special legal privileges not available to other Americans be created for homosexuals? And if so, should we be ready to confer similar privileges upon groups that practice other immoral, socially objectionable, or even illegal behavior? If the gay rights laws sail easily through city council chambers, a quick line could form at the door.

While many focus on the alleged liberating effect of gay rights laws, few people focus on the coercive impact of such statutes. Violations of the gay rights provisions of a Duluth, Minnesota, human rights ordinance (passed over the mayor's veto and later overwhelmingly rescinded in a citizens' repeal effort) led to serious civil liability. Upon showing that a person had violated the ordinance, the court could, among other things, order the defendant to pay compensatory damages for mental anguish or mental suffering in an amount up to three times the amount for all such damages sustained. The reach of the ordinance was so broad that an employer could not have prevented an employee from coming to work "in drag" (wearing the clothes of the opposite sex), since to do so would be to punish a person for "projecting" his "sexual preference and identity."

The combination of a broadly worded ordinance and strong enforcement provisions is the stuff of which legal nightmares are made. Such ordinances give to homosexuals and take away from society at large. They take away, among other things:

•The right of parents or school districts to control the moral caliber of the person who teaches their children.

•The right of an employer to determine whether an applicant's moral character will affect his job performance.

•The right of churches and other religious entities to exclude, or refuse to hire, someone whose lifestyle is contrary to their religious convictions.

Gay rights laws create protections for sexual deviance in ways that cannot be predicted.

Most of the proposed gay rights ordinances technically provide legal protection for more than just homosexuals. They typically provide protection to anyone, regardless of sexual preferences. A literal-minded judge would find that such laws give protection to a large number of sex criminals. Take, for example, the possible protected behaviors under a gay rights ordinance in Alexandria, Virginia:

•A convicted child molester, homosexual or heterosexual, could sue a day-care center that refuses to hire him, claiming discrimination on the basis of his "sexual orientation"; such an ordinance would thus protect behavior declared criminal under state law.

•A motel owner could be sued if he refused to rent a room to an unmarried couple. This would be discrimination in the use of "public accommodations." This would also be discrimination on the basis of "sexual orientation," in this case their sexual preference for unmarried people or for people married to someone else. Such an ordinance would contradict state public policy by protecting behavior declared criminal under state law.

•An insurance company could be sued for refusing to extend health insurance benefits to the sodomy partner of a homosexual or to the wives of a polygamist. The insurance company would be discriminating on the basis of "sexual orientation" by refusing to extend coverage to "spouses" because of their sexual preference. Since both sodomy and polygamy are prohibited under Virginia state law, such an ordinance would protect behavior already declared criminal.

•A landlord who refuses to rent or sell a facility to a person running a house of prostitution could be sued for refusing to rent or sell housing based on the person's "sexual orientation." Yet prostitution is a crime under Virginia law.

•A bank that refuses to loan money to a movie-maker who enjoys making and selling child pornography would be discriminating against the movie-maker on the basis of his "sexual orientation." Yet the making and selling of child pornography is a crime under most state laws.

•Law enforcement officials who arrest the customers of prostitutes, pornography stores, or child sex rings could be sued under the ordinance for "obstruction of practices lawful under this chapter" if it is viewed that the police are discriminating against people who patronize certain "public accommodations" based on their specific "sexual orientation." Prostitution, the sale of pornography, and sex with children are all crimes under state statutes. Such an ordinance could protect behavior declared criminal under state law.

Those who think such results unlikely need only review the surprising interpretations courts give broadly worded laws.

Courts tend to give very restrictive readings to exemptions existing under human rights laws.

Some, but not all, such ordinances contain an exemption for jobs where normal sexual practice might be a "bona fide occupational qualification" (BFOQ). But the applicability of a BFOQ, as civil rights laws prove out, is often dependent on the eye of the beholder. A pastoral position may be one permitting the assertion of a heterosexual BFOQ. But the organist, song leader, or Sunday school superintendent positions would most likely not be. And such exceptions are, in the interpretation of civil rights laws, narrowly construed.

More compelling than the uncertain reach of such ordinances is their effect in coercing men and women of religious conviction to violate their consciences. Gay rights laws declare sexual preference to be amoral. As Dr. Jud Marmor has said, "Moral character is not determined by sexual preference, and individual homosexuals should be evaluated on their own merits and not on the basis of stereotyped behavior."[32]

But homosexual behavior is morally repugnant to a large number of people of varying religious traditions. Such laws might compel churches, religious schools, or other religious organizations to hire persons whose sexual practices contradict their religious doctrines; the laws could force these groups to adopt costly affirmative action programs to hire people who practice behavior they consider sinful. Such laws could force religious organizations that run shelters for battered women and the homeless, soup kitchens, or day-care centers to hire homosexuals in violation of church doctrine, or lose government funding of their operations.

Those who make judgments based on perceived moral character are placed in a hopeless predicament by such laws. The threat of legal sanctions presents such a person with no choice but to violate his conscience or violate the law.

Gay rights, therefore, pose a paradox for society. The creation of novel rights will inevitably create new wrongs: wrongs to religious institutions that seek to use their facilities or hire their employees in accordance with their historic beliefs; wrongs to society by proliferation of a now-accepted behavior that is demonstrably costly to society; wrongs to individuals injured directly or indirectly by homosexual behavior; wrongs to the family structure which is the chief building block of society. Civil rights statutes should continue to prohibit judgments based on color and true status, and to encourage judgments based on character.

Gay rights laws expand homosexual influence.

And one should not understate the change done to society by homosexual influence. When homosexuals are attracted to artistic careers, their influence can be magnified. The artistic director of the famed Minneapolis Children's Theater recently pleaded guilty to criminal sexual conduct for repeated sexual acts with children, over the past decade. His preferences were long known by people in the community, but were widely tolerated because of his influential status. Later, seven other employees of the Children's Theater, all in influential positions, were arrested for sex acts with children.

Through influential people in the media, in fashion, and in the arts, homosexuals project their anti-family, sensual, and unisex ideas onto society and seek to shape it.

The fabric of society is damaged by a subgroup of citizens with serious psychological and medical problems who, because they cannot procreate, must recruit. The ideology associated with a compulsive desire for same-sex sodomy will inevitably shape the way homosexuals see the world, and others will be influenced by that world view. By enacting laws against such behavior in the form of anti-sodomy provisions, society protects parents and children from sodomites, protects potential and incipient homosexuals from themselves, and protects itself from extinction. Furthermore, it teaches all who will listen that sodomy is antithetical to a healthy life-style.

Even the most common sense need to take homosexuality into account is jeopardized by civil rights laws.

In 1977, a young man in Minneapolis presented himself to the Big Brothers organization, which attempts to introduce fatherless boys to men who would make exemplary role models for them. Given the increasing number of single-parent families, Big Brothers organizations throughout the country have experienced an expanding list of mothers who request Big Brothers—men to take their sons fishing, camping, hiking, and to other recreational activities the mother may be unable to provide. The applicant on this day was eager to become a Big Brother.

While reviewing the applicant's resume during the interview, the Big Brothers representative noticed several items that suggested homosexual affiliations. He asked the applicant whether he was a homosexual. The man admitted he was. Despite this revelation, the interview was not terminated. The interviewer mentioned that Big Brothers had a policy of revealing all they knew about potential Big Brothers to the mothers of their clients. Clients had the last word on the suitability of any applicant. It would work the same way with this revelation, the interviewer pointed out. If the mother had no objections to his homosexuality, he would be a Big Brother. It was her "right" either way.

A liberal policy, you might think. But it was not enough for the man who wanted to be a Big Brother. He immediately sued under the Minneapolis gay rights ordinance, alleging that he had been discriminated against as a homosexual. The mere fact that his homosexuality was made known to the mother, he argued, would likely lead to his disqualification as a Big Brother. He was thus being discriminated against for his affectional preference. Big Brothers argued there was nothing discriminatory about this policy. It made no comments, negative or positive, about him. Its representative simply revealed all the facts, just as he would with other protected classes in the human rights law—race, color, age, religion, sex, marital status, and the like. The decision was left up to the mother.

Despite the fair-sounding rationale of Big Brothers, the human rights hearing officer in Minneapolis found Big Brothers guilty of discrimination under the ordinance. Based on that finding, the claimant's lawyer asked for what the law entitled him to: thousands of dollars in costs, the acceptance of the homosexual as part of the organization without disclosing his homosexual preference to mothers of the sons who might go off on weekend outings with him, and "affirmative action," an active solicitation of homosexuals by Big Brothers in the homosexual media. Mixed among the ads soliciting homosexual partners would be advertisements for Big Brothers in Minneapolis, seeking to entice the readership to come to Big Brothers in Minneapolis and be a "big brother" to Minneapolis boys. Before this shoe could drop, Big Brothers brought action in state district court. Although the result was by no means a foregone conclusion, given the vaguely worded ordinance, the judge randomly assigned to the case agreed with Big Brothers and reversed the finding of discrimination. But the case cost the nonprofit organization thousands of dollars. Rather than run the gauntlet again, Big Brothers gave in. They announced in the fall of 1983 that they now have a "national policy of accepting 'gay' men as prospective brothers to fatherless youth, 6-16 years old, unless the man is 'unstable' or has a 'poor life style.' "

Gay rights laws can reach into the sanctity of the private living quarters of a non-homosexual.

More recently, in Madison, Wisconsin, Ann Hacklander and Maureen Rowe were renting an apartment and looking for a roommate to share the expense. When Cari Sprague expressed an interest in living with them and disclosed she was a lesbian, they told her politely they would prefer someone else. Sprague took the matter immediately to the Madison Equal Opportunities Commission (MEOC), an agency charged with enforcement of the Madison gay rights law.

MEOC summoned Hacklander and Rowe to a meeting that proved to be a four-and-a-half-hour self-criticism session. Reduced to tears at the meeting, Hacklander later said she "felt like [she] was in China," not the United States. The result of the meeting was an agreement exacted by MEOC. The two women would pay Sprague fifteen hundred dollars, would attend a sensitivity training class taught by homosexuals, would have their housing situation monitored by MEOC for two years, and would apologize to Sprague in a formal letter. When Rowe, a recent graduate, claimed the settlement would bankrupt her, she was told her bankruptcy was of no consequence to MEOC.

The city council later amended the law so it would not apply to roommate situations, but MEOC continued to lumber along with its case against the two women anyway, knowing that even if Hacklander and Rowe were ultimately to win, they would still have lost in attorney's fees, stress, and time.

These near misses, along with the one direct hit on constitutional liberties, reflect a harsh reality about legal solutions to political problems. They are always, universally, coercive. They start innocently, with theoretical discussions of liberty and equality and end, like the French revolution, with the guillotine. The principle put into practice leads to an inevitable development of case-by-case resolutions that may end with a priest behind bars, a charitable organization wondering whether it ought to close its doors, or some roommates in a college town reduced to tears (and worse) for not wanting to share their apartment with a lesbian.

This is not, of course, a good argument for anarchy. Some issues are so important to the social and political fabric of the country that society tolerates the accompanying coercion. Society is willing to coerce people into keeping their fists off other people's noses and their fingers off other people's wallets. But before society exercises its coercive power to override bona fide religious convictions and historic rights, like the right of a parent to exercise discretion in overseeing the moral character of those who come into contact with her child, there had better be substantial justification. As Abraham Lincoln once said, "What I call liberty is allowing people the maximum freedom in the things they own and the things they do, as long as they do not interfere with the rights of others to do the same."

When it comes to gay rights, therefore, the proponents of such legislation have the burden of proof to show that it is necessary, and it is a heavy burden. From a review of the debates in Congress, in state legislatures, and in city councils, those proponents have yet to make a substantial case.

Making judgments based on character is perfectly legitimate.

The Bible teaches that one of the most important building blocks of good character is to be able to discriminate between good and evil. This quality of discernment tells readers from whom one ought to take advice, with whom one ought to associate, to whom one ought to offer a job. The Christian ought to be able to recognize the adulteress, the fool, the covetous man, the mocker, the reprobate.[33] The erosion of moral boundaries threatens a fundamental and necessary part of good character: being able to separate the precious from the vile. Gay rights laws are the first anti-discrimination laws that prohibit Christians from making necessary moral judgments in forming important life decisions.

CHAPTER 6

THE AMORAL ORTHODOXY:
How Homosexuals Promote the View That Sex Has No Moral Boundaries

6a. "There is nothing wrong with sex. Sex is pleasurable and harmless, unless it is done in a way that is exploitative or coercive."

The logic of gay rights presumes that sex is amoral.

The by now conventional view that there is no right and wrong in sexual expression is a slippery slope. As Prager points out:

> For once one argues that any non-marital form of sexual behavior is as valid as marital sex, the door is opened to *all* other forms of sexual expression. If consensual homosexual activity is valid, why not consensual incest between adults? Why is sex between an adult brother and sister more objectionable than sex between two adult men? If a couple agrees, why not allow consensual adultery? Once non-marital sex is validated, how can we draw any line? Why shouldn't gay liberation be followed by incest liberation?[1]

But the homosexuals are deadly serious about advancing their amoral assault. In mounting this attack, they have devised separate strategies for the different theological traditions. They correctly perceived that the "civil rights" approach would be the perfect vehicle to obtain acceptance from some church groups.

The first to line up behind a gay rights agenda have been those churches and denominations characterized by liberal interpretation of the Bible, churches which do not acknowledge the authority and supremacy of the Bible. In one congressional hearing, for example, the Reverend Cecil Williams was asked whether there were "moral absolutes" which do not change. The Reverend Williams had long been pastor of the Glide Memorial Church in San Francisco, a church that had performed homosexual weddings and caused a major stir in the mid-seventies. Reverend Williams took the liberal view in answer to the question:

> There are no absolutes. All absolutes have to be looked at, criticized, reinterpreted, revised. That is why you have revised versions of the Bible. It is to reestablish, redirect, make relevant, the word in a different time and at a different condition and in different circumstances. That is merely one way of looking at it. There are no absolutes that should not and cannot be reinterpreted and redefined as well as to create different responses for the times during which people live.[2]

By such an interpretation, major social change causes, at least potentially, major theological change. Religion is the tail and common mores are the dog. Pastors reinterpret the Bible to bless a new sociological or political consensus. The church does not stand outside of culture, with an authoritative plumb line, but becomes a facilitator of moral revolution. Such churches quickly acknowledged gay rights efforts and occasionally authorized or participated in demonstrations against churches which preached a Bible-based view of sexuality. Gay rights planks were adopted by the National Council of Churches and the Union of American Hebrew Congregations, among others.

Gay rights activists seek to abandon millennia of moral teaching.

The central religious question spiritually searching people have always faced is, "How can a man be right with God?" The question arises out of our intuition that God is different from us. We are fallible, fumbling, ineffective in our efforts to do right. He is wise, powerful, just. The answer to that question for Christians is to have a radical change of heart. When God's ways cross our ways, when His thoughts cross our thoughts, it is our imperative to change, to acknowledge our wrong, and to ask God's help to become right.

> **6b. "We must appreciate our differences and stop looking down on people who do things differently. Christians should recognize that there is nothing inherently better or worse about homsexuality or heterosexuality."**

Accepting homosexual sodomy as normal damages the authority of the Bible and dishonors the social fabric.

Put simply, to those who believe that the Bible is the Word of God, homosexuality is immoral because God says so. But even were there no explicit command in the Bible that forbade sodomy, it is easy to show that it is an unnatural act—whether by examining basic anatomy, hygiene, the physical and psychological consequences for the homosexuals themselves, the promiscuity and exploitation built into "normal" homosexual behavior, or by merely a head count of the world's religions. To ignore that reality, to pretend out of misguided compassion that homosexuals are to celebrate their sodomy, does incalculable moral damage.

To the extent such theology becomes embodied in law, it damages the social fabric. Most reasonable people reject the old nostrum that "you can't legislate morality." They realize that law is nothing but a statement of minimum public morality that teaches members of society a basic course in right and wrong. The law is society's "schoolmaster." The repeal of laws against sodomy, together with the creation of special homosexual privileges, teaches that homosexual behavior is a valid alternative lifestyle, and lures others to experiment with a destructive perversion.

> **6c. "Using the cultural prejudices of the Bible to endorse homophobia is un-Christian. New Testament condemnations of homosexuality reflect cultural prejudice and don't address loving, committed homosexual relationships."**

To reject the Bible's teaching on homosexuality as merely culturally based is to deny biblical authority on sexual morality.

The cultural argument is the final refuge of those who wish to avoid a clear command of the Bible. When the Bible is clear, and its interpretation is self-evident, one opposing biblical standard can support that Scripture writers were limited by their upbringing and cultural milieu. Such limitations, they argue, make it necessary to disregard commands that manifest such cultural bias.

Such a view, if accepted generally, would eliminate the authority of the Bible entirely. Who is to say that the prohibition of adultery was not a cultural byproduct of ancient biases before people discovered the benefits of "swinging"? In fact, sexuality and its physical expression are close to the core of Christian teaching. The ideal of Christian marriage exists from creation onward and takes its greatest novelty from its use as a model of the relationship between Christ and the church.[3] Commands to sexual purity saturate biblical ethics from Genesis to Revelation. Its counterpart, any sexual immorality outside of marriage, leads a number of lists of sins especially reprehensible.

The Bible teaches that even consensual homosexuality is a proper subject for legal regulation.

Because homosexuality is an offense against nature as well as against revealed religion, it is properly legislated against by lawmakers. There is no authority in the Bible for legislating faith in Jesus Christ or requiring acts of worship. That would make conversion meaningless. But laws against homosexual acts are not only permissible, but they embody one of the fundamental purposes of law. As Paul says in 1 Timothy 1:8-11, laws prohibiting homosexuality are genuine expressions of the purpose of law itself. Lumping homosexuality together with murder, slave trading, and other serious crimes, he says that the law "is not made for a righteous man, but for the lawless and disobedient."

6d. "The Bible does not condemn committed, loving relationships between people of the same sex."

The Bible could not be clearer in its condemnation of homosexual behavior.

No matter how plain the words, many theologians have "reexamined" the Bible on this subject and come up with some revisionist—indeed astonishing—conclusions. Like those who reexamine historical documents and find that Hitler was innocent, that Lee Harvey Oswald was railroaded, and that Alger Hiss was patriotic, those who believe that the "Bible nowhere condemns homosexuality" face a daunting assignment. There is some major explaining away to do. It is a familiar pattern: worldly culture leads the way (feminism, Marxism, homosexuality) and compliant theologians follow, explaining how "keep silent" means "speak," "do not steal" means "forcibly redistribute income," and "abomination" means "live and let live." Homosexuals recognize the political dimensions of theological controversies. If "guerrilla theater" and propaganda can influence scientists to repeal their findings, cannot the same tactics dilute accepted doctrine or foster new church teaching?

What does the Bible say?

Therefore God also gave them up to uncleanness through the lusts of their own hearts, to dishonor their own bodies between themselves: who changed the truth of God into a lie, and worshipped and served the creature more than the Creator, who is blessed for ever. Amen.

For this cause God gave them up unto vile affections: for even their women did change the natural use into that which is against nature: and likewise also the men, leaving the natural use of the woman, burned in their lust one toward another; men with men working that which is unseemly, and receiving in themselves that recommence of their error which was meet.

*And even as they did not like to retain God in their knowledge,
God gave them over to a reprobate mind, to do those things
which are not convenient* (Romans 1:24-28).

On its face, this biblical view of homosexual behavior could not
be clearer. It is quite simply an "abomination." Because men turn from
God to worship humanistic inventions, God gives them up to unnatural
lusts that devastate them, spiritually and physically. The apostle Paul
similarly counsels the Corinthians not to deceive themselves:
Homosexual offenders will not inherit the kingdom of God unless they
repent (1 Corinthians 6:9-10). Jude paints a picture worth a thousand
words: The sulfurous barrenness of the south shore of the Dead Sea, the
only residue of once-flourishing Sodom and Gomorrah, gives God's
most dramatic statement on a culture given to homosexuality (verse 7).

These are only a few of the numerous condemnations of sodomy
in the Bible. Fifteen scriptural terms characterize or identify the sin of
sodomy, among them:

- abomination (Leviticus 18:22)
- lusts (Romans 1:24)
- wicked (Genesis 13:13)
- vile affections (Romans 1:26)
- against nature (Romans 1:26)
- unseemly (Romans 1:27)
- strange flesh (Jude 7)
- reprobate mind (Romans 1:28)
- dogs [homosexual prostitutes] (Deuteronomy 23:18).

Rejecting the biblical view, based on "compassion," is not compassionate.

The revisionist theology is far from compassionate. It is cruel to
homosexuals. The sodomite is trapped in a lust that is destroying him
by inches and yards. To tell him he cannot help himself, to tell him to

rejoice in his fatal disease, is to consign him forever to unhappiness. Much better the simple message of Christian grace: You are a responsible moral being who has sinned grievously against God. God loves you but hates your lifestyle. You are headed for judgment, but there is a way out.

Trendy pronouncements on homosexuality by religious bureaucracies are ill-informed and are not based on clear Bible teaching.

A variety of statements by religious groups reflect this trend. For example, one mainline denomination has addressed the topic in a brochure titled, *Resources for Ministry*:

Certainly the Bible does condemn lustful, exploitative and dehumanizing sexual behavior—both homosexual and heterosexual. However, nowhere are loving committed relationships between persons of the same gender condemned.... Today, gay Christians and their non-gay supporters affirm homosexuality as a gift of God to be celebrated just like the gift of heterosexual orientation.[4]

The "Social Justice Committee" of the Minnesota Council of Churches, an ecumenical body composed of most of the mainline denominations in the state, adopted a similar statement on homosexuality. It said in part:

God's intended wholeness includes human sexuality as a gift for the expression of love and the generation of life.... There may be creative and whole expressions of one's sexuality at various levels in relationships between men and women, between men and other men, and between women and other women. We seek to enable persons to understand and to act out their sexuality in ways which are life-giving to themselves and to other persons with whom they are in relationship.[5]

The statement goes on to condemn an attitude that views homosexuality as "something to hide or exorcise" rather than "something to celebrate." Homosexuals "are best understood as a 'people who have been sinned against.'"

Such views are not the exclusive province of liberal church groups. In *An Evangelical Look at Homosexuality*, Ralph Blair, a member of the National Association of Evangelicals, says:

> Part of the task of evangelicals is to abandon unbiblical crusades against homosexuality and to help those who have quite naturally developed along homosexual lines to accept themselves as Christ accepted them—just as they are and to live lives which include responsible homosexual behavior.[6]

In *Sex for Christians*, Fuller Theological Seminary professor Lewis Smedes recommends "optimum homosexual morality"—that is, a permanent, "non-exploitative" relationship between homosexuals who "can manage neither change nor celibacy."[7] In *The Sexual Revolution*, a Dutch pastor calls for evangelicals to develop a "viable homosexual ethic" calling for "permanent relationships between unchangeable homosexuals."[8]

To say that homosexuals cannot be changed is uninformed. To say they will lovingly limit their perverted practices to one person is naive. But to say that the Bible approves of all this is ludicrous.

The word to describe homosexuality in the Old Testament is a very strong one, toevah, "abomination." It conveys great repugnance and implies the strongest possible moral judgment. It is typically listed with child sacrifice as the two characteristic "abominations" that were practiced by the Canaanites. It was viewed as such a unique threat that God promised to "vomit" the people out of the land if they committed these offenses.[9]

6e. "God loves gay people, too."

God loves people, but hates the sin that destroys people.

The Bible says, of course, that God loves the world so much that He gave His only son to die for it. That world includes homosexuals as well as heterosexuals. It also includes liars and frauds and cheats and racists and the smugly self-righteous. To say that God loves the world and the people in it does not mean that He approves of their behavior.

6f. "Jesus never condemned homosexuality."

Jesus spoke of Old Testament moral law as authoritative.

This proves too much. He also did not condemn drug abuse or child molesting. Or, for that matter, rape. The fact that He didn't need to shows how clearly established the principle was.

6g. "The Church has always taught that sex is sinful."

Not so. The Bible speaks at great length about sensual love.

People who make this claim simply have not read the Bible. The Song of Solomon contains the most beautiful description of marital love in all of literature. In 1 Corinthians 7:5, the apostle Paul instructs married couples, "Do not deprive each other (sexually) except by mutual consent and for a time, so that you may devote yourselves to prayer. Then come together again..." Indeed, the family, and with it procreation, have from the days of Adam and Eve been held in special honor by Christians.

6h. "Doesn't the Bible say we should judge not lest we be judged?"

Christians are obligated to make wise and discerning judgments on behavior.

It does. We are unable, as human beings, to come to any ultimate judgment with respect to people. But we can judge their acts. Indeed, we are obligated to do so. It is not our job to be the eternal judge of a criminal, but we can say his criminal activity is wrong.

6i. "The Old Testament references used against gay sex are taken out of context and usually were part of ceremonial laws that, if we obeyed them, would have us all refusing to wear certain fabrics and not shaving our beards."

The prohibition of sodomy is not "ceremonial" but moral.

Old Testament law contains enduring moral elements and ceremonial elements that Christians believe were fulfilled in Christ and are no longer operative. Leviticus has both kinds of prohibitions. Among its restrictions on ceremonial uncleanness are clearly moral proscriptions of "abominations." The commands against adultery are not irrelevant just because the commands against eating with unwashed hands are. The moral commands still endure. The term for homosexual sex in Leviticus ("abominations") is the strongest of Hebrew condemnations.

The prohibitions of sodomy in Leviticus are universal. There are no exceptions.

It is equally untrue to say that the Bible only forbids homosexual activity by priests, and hence its prohibitions, like the ceremonial law, have disappeared. As a part of the Levitical law, some would say, the regulations of Leviticus 18 are no longer in effect. They were for one group (priests) and one time (the old dispensation).

The rule in question was not for the priests alone. It is explicitly directed to the priests *to teach the people*. Moreover, biblical condemnations of homosexuality occur both before (Sodom) and after the law (the New Testament). Those strong prohibitions make clear that homosexuality is a moral matter, going to the very core of creation and human sexuality.

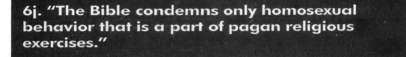

6j. "The Bible condemns only homosexual behavior that is a part of pagan religious exercises."

The Bible makes no qualification to its prohibition of homosexual acts.

The abominable thing about men lying with men, the argument goes, is not the physical act. It is the connection of homosexual acts to male temple prostitutes, luring Jews to pagan worship condemned by God. Jews venturing into sexual acts with pagan prostitutes were surrendering their loyalty to the one God.

Nowhere is the Leviticus prohibition on homosexual conduct limited to religious prostitution any more than it limits the prohibition against bestiality to sex with beasts owned by foreigners. It simply forbids men lying with men (18:22).

6k. "The incident of Sodom shows how people misunderstand what the Bible says about sexual relationships."

God's judgment on Sodom is a condemnation of the behavior for which Sodom was known.

Some say the real offense that triggered the fire and brimstone in Sodom and Gomorrah was inhospitality.[10] Some go further and say that those who do not receive practicing homosexuals into the ministry in the church are guilty of the sin of Sodom and Gomorrah, not the sodomites themselves. They are being "inhospitable."

It is true, to be sure, that those seeking to sodomize the heavenly visitors were guilty of breaching the important code of hospitality in the ancient Near East. That breach of etiquette no doubt aggravated the offense. Sodom was inhospitable to the visitors, but the sin that buried them beneath the wrath of God was pride and sensuality illustrated by abominable sexual behavior.

The Sodomites' sin was their desire for carnal knowledge of the angelic visitors.

Others say that the men of Sodom only wanted to "get to know" the angels. They try to support the inhospitality theory by arguing that the men of Sodom only wanted to become acquainted with Lot's visitors. Their disappointing and ultimately futile efforts to interrupt the social gathering caused God's judgment to fall.

The argument is linguistically untenable. Their intent was no different from that of the Benjamites in Judges 19:22-25, who settled for a woman only when there were no men available. The linguistic difficulties facing this revisionist view are compounded by the New Testament's interpretation of why Sodom fell. According to Jude 7, Sodom fell because of "fornication and going after strange flesh." The idea that the men of Sodom had in mind a competitive tea party is not consistent with the Genesis account and its tone of sensual desperation, not to mention the actual words of the narrative.

61. "True Christianity is compassionate. It is summed up in love. It doesn't seek to change people; it accepts them."

Love means helping people gain freedom from self-destructive behavior.

Anyone who has dealt with compulsive exhibitionists, sitting forlorn after being arrested for exposing themselves, knows the terrible shame they experience. Wrestling with a strange compulsion they find almost impossible to control, they expose themselves in public libraries or on street corners, then appear in court too ashamed to talk about their escapades to court-appointed lawyers. It is one thing to feel compassion for them. It is quite another to join with them in a parade down Fifth Avenue to St. Patrick's Cathedral, dressed in raincoats and carrying placards celebrating "Flashers' Pride." All decent people applaud the Augustine who repents from his hedonistic lifestyle and lives a life of Christian purity. But a publicly celebrated "Adulterers' Pride Day" should be viewed with contempt.

Public officials nonetheless often rush to be identified with "Gay Pride," to show "compassion." No one should take pride in his own immoral behavior, but is it not worse to encourage another to take pride in behavior that is destroying him?

Real compassion sometimes says, "change."

Real compassion gives the right prescription. The Bible talks of *repentance*, a word that suggests to some modern minds the hairshirted prophet bearing the solemn placard, "Repent!" It sounds like an antiquated concept, the stuff of Puritan caricatures.

But there is much sound theology and freedom in that single word. It suggests that there is a standard of right and wrong that does not change with changing mores. It suggests that those standards are as enduring as scientific laws which govern natural phenomena. Hidden within that word also is the idea that such standards are not only absolute, but good. When Moses gave his parting admonition to the nation of Israel, he told the people that he was setting before them life and death, blessings and cursings, and advised them to "choose life" (Deuteronomy 30:11-20). The moral law that God has established for His creatures is both good and life-giving; one departs from that standard at risk to his own life, health, and happiness.

Repent means, therefore, that a person must have a "change of mind" that brings his ideas into conformity with God's expressed directions for how to live a happy, healthy, and wholesome life. It means that one ought to repent not only as a sign of obedience to God and His will, but also for the good of his own life and future. It means also that he can repent, no matter how firm and unyielding the grip of sin and disorder may be on his life. A command given by a wise and good law-giver implies the ability to comply with it.

The formula the apostle Paul used in the public assembly and in his house-to-house visitation was, "Repentance toward God and faith in our Lord Jesus Christ." Repentance acknowledges the standard and our willingness to accept it. Faith in the Lord Jesus Christ means to acknowledge that he was God's anointed messenger from heaven who shared the human condition. Through his death and resurrection, He was confirmed as Lord and life-giver, who is willing to save and sanctify those who acknowledge Him. This mystery of conversion fills a person with new power to overcome both the penalty of sin and its power. "If any man be in Christ," the Bible says, "he is a new creature."[11]

That transformation is never easy. It is not easy for the homosexual. It is not easy for the glutton, the materialist, the adulterer, the thief, the proud man, or any other of us with our peculiar besetting sins. But it is possible.

Genuine Christians love homosexuals and see them as made in the image of God.

For the true Christian, the homosexual is not a moral pariah to declaim against. He is like the lost sheep, the lost coin, or the lost son depicted in three of Jesus' parables (Luke 15). The Christian, while condemning the homosexual movement for its false ideology, looks—as Jesus did—at the individual. The homosexual is the lost sheep who unwittingly has wandered away from the flock and exposed himself to serious and destructive dangers. The Christian longs to seek him out and bring him back with rejoicing.

As pitiable as a lost sheep, as precious as the lost silver coin, the homosexual needs to be found. The Christian wants to be as diligent as the woman looking to restore that lost silver coin to the other nine on her bridal necklace. The homosexual is of great worth.

Finally, the homosexual has the potential of the lost son. The lost son, having wasted his inheritance through enormous prodigality, is reduced to eating filthy husks of corn with the swine. But in his father's eye, he can be washed clean, wear a new robe, put on shoes and a ring of acceptance. So the homosexual has the potential to be a pure and attractive picture of Christ's power. He has the potential that every sinner has to be right in the eyes of God. The Christian, therefore, must be like the waiting father, ready to accept and embrace the truly repentant homosexual.[12]

Conventional wisdom tells us that to tolerate weakness is often a virtue; to encourage immorality is always a vice. Gay rights laws that give special protections and privileges to people who practice sexual perversion are little more than a reward for immorality.

CHAPTER 7

THE AVOIDANCE FACTOR:
*What Homosexuals Must Cover Up About
Typical Same-Sex Lifestyles*

**7a. "Don't use homophobic stereotypes. Judge
us individually. You can't generalize about any
group."**

*To evaluate gay rights proposals, one must examine the reality of
homosexual behavior.*

To understand whether gay rights laws make sense for society, we
have to understand first who the gays are. The legitimacy of claims
against the rest of society can only be evaluated properly when we
have defined and described who is making them. Here, as always, it is
important to separate the image from the reality. The visitor at Wild
West Village in Knott's Berry Farm can become so enchanted with the
weather-worn wood, the dusty streets, and the smell of gunpowder that
he altogether loses his orientation in time and space and never looks
behind the elaborate facade. It is equally easy to lose perspective on
public policy issues, to look merely at the carefully constructed image
of the modern homosexual culture without examining the hard reality
lurking behind the colorful exteriors.

Because demands for gay rights have profound social consequences, it is legitimate to examine the nature of "gayness" thoroughly
before rushing to embrace it simply because it comes under the familiar and popular banner of equal rights. For many years, nearly all
homosexuals remained in the closet, concealing their behavior from
employers, from friends, even from spouses. Many wrestled against
their impulses in much the same way an exhibitionist wrestles against
the compulsive behavior that makes him feel guilty and ashamed.

Such quiet, closeted, often tormented homosexuals rightfully evoke compassion from those who come to know their plight and would like to help them out of it. But these are not the people for whom the gay rights laws are primarily designed or who actively lobby for them. Because they keep their sexuality private, they are seldom, if ever, discriminated against. Content to stay outside the political arena, they are a group distinct from the militant homosexuals who want public acceptance and legal sanction, not just private tolerance, for their lifestyle.

The militant homosexual community has sought to overcome the natural revulsion their behavior triggers by efforts to polish their image, efforts that have been largely successful. They have won the support of many people of good will—including prominent religious and political leaders—by identifying themselves as an oppressed minority calling for social justice. These leaders range from denominational leaders of major religious groups to a coalition of people who have been historical supporters of causes associated with civil rights. Books have regularly appeared to enlist, by firm or flimsy evidence, great historical and literary figures in the homosexual camp. Bachelorhood, accusations of enemies, ambiguous references in sonnets, or genuine same-sex friendships are commonly the extent of "evidence" offered to "establish" contributions made by homosexuals to society.[1] Homosexuals often express an interest in intellectual movements and the arts, a worldly sophistication, and a love for fashion. Some militants suggest the spiritual or intellectual love of same-sex partners is preferable to the more pedestrian "breeding" of heterosexuals. Most of all, they want their lifestyle to be seen as "gay," free from slavery to conventional rules, exuberant, full of zest, and suffused with commitment to loving, caring, and sharing relationships. As one clinical psychiatrist summed up the modern homosexual message: "See how uninhibited we are, see how we've thrown off the chains of guilt—unlike you poor straight people who have for so long subjected us to feelings of worthlessness and sinfulness."[2]

Homosexual militants seek to, but cannot, deny the unsettling facts of the homosexual experience.

When homosexuals challenge facts and generalizations, they rarely say which facts, or cite their own. They issue blanket denunciations—"These are all the old lies and distortions people have used for years to justify their bigotry." We all want to be factual, so perhaps we can request enlightenment:

a. How many partners does the median male homosexual have? Are you saying that the Center for Disease Control was wrong when it used the 500 number? What should it have been? Was the study that the median AIDS patient had had a thousand partners in error?[3] What do you think the right number would be?

b. When *Atlantic Monthly* published an article suggesting that homosexuals were responsible for over fifty per cent of the cases of syphilis in this country, do you agree? What is an appropriate number? Why is the homosexual population so infested with venereal disease?

c. Are the kind of "homoerotic" practices pictured by Robert Mapplethorpe in his famous exhibit, representative of the homosexual community? Are the mutilations, physical abuses, ingestion of excrement and the like shown there the kind of behaviors you believe should be protected from social stigma?

7b. "Gay people are not different in their behavior from other people."

Homosexual practices are often astonishing to normal people.

To make an assessment of this claim, one must know what homosexuals do, where they do it, and with whom they do it. Homosexuals typically engage in oral or anal sodomy, or mutual masturbation, with members of the same sex. Frustrated by the biological impossibility of natural sexual relations between members of the same sex, homosexuals must use body apertures not constructed for sexual penetration or bring their mouth into contact with areas designed for the elimination of human waste, either of which causes serious hygienic and health risks.[4]

Once the natural reluctance to come into contact with human waste is broken down, a significant proportion of homosexuals go further. Some homosexuals, such as the famous psychologist and sexologist Havelock Ellis, are urolagniacs, ingesting the urine and feces of their partners.[5] Although homosexuals have no monopoly on bizarre sexual practices, their initial attraction to unnatural acts draws them in disproportionate numbers to more widely known practices such as sadism and masochism, and less widely known fisting and rimming.[6]

Homosexuals also practice other forms of deviant behavior. One book reports that one-fifth of all homosexuals admit to having sexual contact, or at least masturbating with, animals.[7] A prominent homosexual, Charley Shively, wrote an article for *Fag Rag* titled "Bestiality as an Act of Revolution," and *The Gay Report,* a widely read and much praised book in the homosexual community, reports positive testimonials with no apparent shame and no adverse comment from those having sex with Labrador retrievers, cows, and horses: "My first sexual experience...was...with a cow—not bad, but boys are better."[8] Most homosexuals have had some experience with oral-anal sex, sadomasochism, group orgies, bondage, or transvestism.[9] One of the perverse practices spreading throughout the country is the use of gerbils, inserted into the rectum of the partner, a practice described in *The Sexual Dead-End,* by Stephen Green.[10] Hospital emergency rooms need to perform gerbilectomies in areas where the practice has become fashionable. Should this practice be protected from any social stigma?

Homosexuals often have an interest in public or quasi-public sex.

Unlike the heterosexual, the male homosexual often practices his sexual behavior outside the privacy of his own bedroom. *Gayellow*

Pages, a reference book widely circulated in the homosexual community, gives a state-by-state, city-by-city description of where homosexuals congregate and for what purpose. Letter codes reflect what is available: anal sex, oral sex, sadomasochism, and a bewildering variety of other perverse behaviors. Several books have described the phenomenon, and *The Gay Report* takes it as a given:

> It is generally well known that male homosexuals often perform sex outside the home. John Rechy's books, especially *Numbers* and *The Sexual Outlaw*, document the lives of sex hunters of city streets and parks. The use of public toilets for cruising and sex is so well known that a technical book by Cornell University entitled *The Bath Room* includes a whole section discussing the homosexual issue in the design of modern public restrooms.... Psychiatrists have on occasion suggested that men choose public places because they find the danger attractive. Most contemporary gay writers, however, indicate that sex in public places is chosen for its convenience or its anonymity or both, and a few have even suggested that there is something revolutionary about both promiscuity and public sex.[11]

Frequent places mentioned for homosexual behavior are public restrooms at bus stations, service stations, shopping malls, public libraries, or rest stops (where visitors sometimes cut out circular "glory holes" in the partitions between the stalls for anonymous sex); public parks, such as areas in Golden Gate Park in San Francisco, where groups gather in the bushes according to their deviant specialty; beaches, where at designated times sodomites meet for furtive sexual activity; public baths or "health clubs," where groups gather around to watch others engage in sodomy or retire to private booths for one of a number of perverted acts; gay bars and nightclubs where homosexuals "cruise" each other, looking for short, ten-minute stands, often in the restrooms; street corners, where standing or signaling has special meaning for those cruising by in automobiles; and pornographic bookstores, peep shows, or movie houses, where small cubicles or lounge areas are used for sodomy or masturbation.[12]

Dr. Charles Socarides, a leading psychiatric expert on homosexuality, gives the flavor of such public liaisons: "Often the homosexual encounters consist of no more than a quick orgasm induced by two males grasping each other's genitals in the anonymous setting of a public toilet or darkened doorway."[13]

The baths in particular reveal much about homosexual practices:

The degree of promiscuity in the baths defies the imagination of those not familiar with homosexuality. From the point of view of traditional values, they are probably some of the most destructive and degrading institutions in America today. There is no indication, however, that any of the homosexual organizations has opposed or in any way showed interest in counteracting the effects of the baths. From the medical point of view, the baths probably constitute a major focus for the transmission of disease.[14]

Homosexuals often engage in startling promiscuity.

Some homosexuals, of course, live desperately lonely lives, punctuated by occasional and furtive sexual behavior that leaves them feeling guilty and ashamed. Others commit such acts only in their tortured imaginations. A few (many of them women) maintain, at least for a time, a longer-term relationship with one partner. But these occasional practitioners are, according to recent statistical data, dwarfed by their more promiscuous brethren.

Until recently, the staggering promiscuity of the homosexual community was only dimly appreciated by the statisticians. A survey reported in the official publication of the American Public Health Association, for example, said that over a lifetime the typical homosexual has forty-nine different sexual partners and that between eight and twelve percent of homosexuals have more than five hundred partners during their lifetime.

Those numbers, though huge by heterosexual standards, appear now to be the tip of the iceberg. A fact long known within the homosexual community was unveiled to the public only recently with the fearful spread of a new disease. During the course of research on AIDS, it was discovered that the typical homosexual interviewed had over five hundred different sexual partners. The AIDS victims considered by themselves averaged eleven hundred different sexual partners; some reported as many as twenty thousand.[15] Other reports showed that some homosexuals had as many as nine short sexual encounters in one evening at a bath or bar. One homosexual reported, "I believe my estimate of 4,000 sex partners to be very accurate. I have been actively gay since I was 13 (thirty-one years ago). An average of two or three new partners per week is not excessive, especially when one considers that I will have ten to twelve partners during one night at the baths."[16]

Prostitution is a particularly common experience among homosexuals.

Prostitution, like child abuse, is not the exclusive preserve of homosexuals. But while a minority of heterosexuals use prostitutes, or have used them on occasion, few older, active homosexuals live without them. Many psychologists have pointed out the preoccupation of these homosexuals with youthful, lithe bodies.[17] Such a preoccupation is, to be sure, not foreign to heterosexuals either. But while the heterosexual couple grows older together, the homosexual seeks sex in the same young age group, even as he ages. When he begins to lose his attractiveness, he has no choice but to buy sex. That need has given rise to a subculture of prostitution by boys and young men in the inner city.[18]

Wherever any concentration of homosexuals exists, there exists of necessity young male prostitutes. Every time a cruising homosexual picks up another boy for exploitation, another victim is created. One leading homosexual magazine describes without condemnation the scene on a boulevard in Los Angeles known for underage prostitution:

> Seemingly undaunted...literally hundreds of hustlers flock to
> "S and M" boulevard every week. Sometimes the atmosphere

is tense with competition...but for the most part an air of camaraderie prevails, assisted by the widespread belief that however plentiful the supply of hustlers, the demand is almost always greater.[19]

There is always widespread prostitution in the homosexual community. *The Advocate* shows the breadth of homosexual prostitution when it carries ads for "escort services"—as many as four hundred per issue. One observer estimated the total number of homosexual prostitutes in the United States at no fewer than seventy thousand. Another author estimated there are three hundred thousand boy prostitutes in the United States.[20]

The emphasis on youth and beauty, in a community without long-term monogamous commitment, leads inevitably to merchandising of sex as a commodity. One former homosexual describes his previous lifestyle:

> It was a sordid life. As you get older, anything good about homosexuality passes away and you are left with all of the bad things. You no longer are attractive and you cannot make contact. You have to pay for any sex you get. And then there is no involvement, there is no love. No friendship is involved; just a business transaction. So the rejection of the homosexual life is very intense.[21]

Homosexuals have a disproportionate number of pedophiles.

Although hotly contested by the homosexual community, substantial evidence indicates that homosexuals are also sexually involved with children. Some heterosexuals share the perverted practice, to be sure, but homosexuals have become increasingly open about it.[22] Since the decadent Romans wrote two millennia ago about the attractions of man-boy love, observers have noted linkages between homosexuality and pedophilia. The most prominent—and presumably most responsible—homosexuals, such as economist John Maynard Keynes, have sought out excursions to places where, as he put it, he could enjoy "bed and boy."[23] The Gay Teachers Association has demanded the right to teach students that "gay is proud" and provide sexual "counseling."[24] New York homosexual teachers agreed that homosexual relationships with their students were improper, but reserved the right to have homosexual relations with other children outside the classroom.[25] Prominent homosexual activists and organizations have a stated objective to remove age-of-consent laws from state statutes, permitting voluntary sex with minors (see chapter 3). Los Angeles public schools have seen the introduction of Project 10 which, among other things, refers teenagers confused about their sexuality to homosexual counselors.

The coming out of the homosexual has also made public certain subgroups of the homosexual community. Homosexuals with tastes for interracial promiscuity founded "Black and White Men Together" (BWMT). The Eulenspiegel Society was formed for homosexuals drawn toward sadomasochism and perverse dominant/submissive sexual acts. The Eulenspiegel Society announced society meetings on "how to conduct a scene with a beginning masochist" and on "tattooing and dominant/submissive sex."[26]

A survey done by two homosexual authors revealed that three-fourths of homosexuals had at some time had sex with boys sixteen to nineteen or younger. One reported, "My lover and I are into young boys 13-18 years old.... I am actively involved with many of them insofar as the social services, family courts, schools, probation departments, etc. are concerned." Another said, "How long will we boy lovers have to wait? How long before we can walk honestly and proudly hand in hand with our young friends and not have to palm them off as our nephews or our stepsons?"[27]

One prominent homosexual activist told a group of educators that the homosexual has every right to influence children: "It is absurd to hire a teacher and then say 'But don't bring yourself to work. Don't bring your values or world view into the classroom.' "[28]

The interest in children by homosexual activists is reflected in this quotation from a speech at a North American Man/Boy Love Association meeting in Minneapolis: "There's not a boy out there...who does not need oral sex right now. I have never met a boy who did not enjoy being given oral sex."[29]

NAMBLA says it is "strongly opposed to age of consent laws and other restrictions which deny adults and youth the full enjoyment of their bodies and control over their lives." NAMBLA's goal is to end the long-standing oppression of men and boys involved in any mutually consensual relationship by 1) building a support network for such men and boys; 2) educating the public on the benevolent nature of man/boy love; 3) aligning with the lesbian, gay, and other movements for sexual liberation; and 4) supporting the liberation of persons of all ages from sexual prejudice and oppression.[30]

But such an interest is not limited to a lunatic fringe of homosexuals. Regrettably, prominent leaders have sexually used children. Perhaps the brightest judge on the Minnesota District Court bench, a Harvard Law School graduate, had to be removed from the bench for homosexual prostitution with minors.[31] A nationally celebrated artistic director in the children's theater movement was convicted a few years ago for repeated acts of child molestation, along with several of his associates. His conviction followed that of a prominent Minneapolis high school music teacher who repeatedly videotaped perverted sexual acts of minors, many of them his own students. And a superficial review of mainstream homosexual newspapers reveals advertisements such as the following:

> I'm wanting to establish a friendship with a 16-18 year old, affectionate, gentle personality with a good sense of humor who would enjoy movies, breakfasts, music, skinny dipping, or biking with a clean, honest and caring 34-year-old male. Racial and economic background are not discriminating factors; no smoke or drugs, however.[32]

Such ads are not confined to the homosexual media. The

Minneapolis Star several years ago carried an ad on its church page from a local homosexual church featuring a boy dressed only in shorts. It offered prizes and cash awards for homosexual adolescents who would come to a meeting at the church with examples of homosexual art or prose.

7c. "Gay people have no more physical or psychological problems than anyone else."

Homosexual behavior has deleterious medical consequences.

Homosexual behavior leads to problems far beyond the circle of homosexuals themselves. As a group, homosexuals release both disease and crime into society to an extent far in excess of their percentage of the population.[33] The connection between homosexuals and ill health has been underscored most recently by the rise of AIDS.

Prior to this disease, however, the medical community had long known the medical effects of homosexuality. The high rate of illness in the homosexual community is legendary. One survey revealed that seventy-eight percent of homosexuals have been affected at least once by a sexually transmitted disease (STD), and that a large number of homosexuals have been afflicted with illnesses such as urethritis, hepatitis, herpes, pediculosis, scabies, venereal warts, and intestinal parasites.[34]

Medical specialists know the disproportionate impact such diseases are having on the homosexual community. Although homosexuals represent five percent or less of the U.S. population, they are responsible for half of the nation's cases of syphilis and a "phenomenal incidence of venereal disease" generally.[35] Syphilis, once thought under control, has recently burst into a new epidemic with a nationwide increase of twenty-three percent in the first six months of 1987 over the first six months of 1986, and a 105 percent increase over the same period in New York City alone.[36] Homosexuals also carry slightly more than half of the cases of gonorrhea of the throat and of intestinal infections.[37]

Homosexual behaviors have public health consequences.

Diseased homosexual food handlers in public restaurants have been responsible for major outbreaks of amebiasis and hepatitis A infections in San Francisco and Minneapolis; homosexuals have a rate of infectious hepatitis B twenty to fifty times greater than heterosexual males, and significantly higher rates of hepatitis A.[38] Some studies show that between one-half and three-fourths of homosexual men have or have had hepatitis B.[39] Ninety percent of homosexually active men demonstrate chronic or recurrent viral infections with herpes virus, CMV, and hepatitis B.[40] It is no wonder that Dr. Selma Dritz, an official of the San Francisco Department of Public Health, wrote that "special precautions are required to protect the public from [disease carriers] who work as food handlers, bartenders, attendants in medical care facilities, and as teachers and aids in day-care centers for infants and young children."[41]

During the first decade that gay rights laws were in effect in San Francisco, the city saw a sharp increase in the venereal disease rate to twenty-two times the national average. Over a ten-year period, the annual rate of infectious hepatitis A increased 100 percent; infectious hepatitis B, 300 percent; and amoebic colon infections increased 2,500 percent. Venereal disease clinics in the city saw seventy-five thousand patients every year during the same decade, of whom close to eighty percent were homosexual males. Twenty percent of them carried rectal gonorrhea.[42]

Homosexuals are often the victims of exotic infections.

Homosexuals also have a group of rare bowel diseases, usually thought to be limited to the tropics. These are generally lumped together under the designation "gay bowel syndrome."[43] Because many male homosexuals ingest fecal matter, it is estimated that up to one-half have contracted parasitic amebiasis, a disease of the colon caused by parasites. One public official found forty percent of homosexual men attending sexually transmitted disease clinics had the problem.[44] It is no wonder that the *New York Times Magazine* makes the following statement: "Bizarre infections are so common in the homosexual community that one scientist, presenting a report on these occurrences...called his talk 'Manhattan: The Tropical Isle.' "[45]

Such statistics do not come about by accident or bad luck. The physiology of the rectum makes it clear that sodomy is unnatural. The inward expansion of the rectum during anal intercourse frequently tears the rectal lining, resulting in spasms, colitis, cramps, and a variety of other physical responses.[46] Furthermore, sperm can readily penetrate the rectal wall (the vagina cannot be so penetrated) and do massive immunological damage, leaving the body vulnerable to a bewildering variety of opportunistic infections.[47] Simply put, homosexual practices are unhealthy.

AIDS in this country has been transmitted primarily through homosexual sex.

The perilous combination of a disease-ridden population and incredible promiscuity has led to the proliferation of AIDS and has brought all these facts to public attention. Bursting into prominence in 1981, AIDS (Acquired Immune Deficiency Syndrome) soon had caused more fatalities than Legionnaires' disease and toxic shock syndrome combined. It was initially named GRID (Gay Related Immune Deficiency disease), but whatever its acronym, it proved lethal. Fewer than 14 percent of AIDS victims have survived more than three years; no victim is known to have ever fully recovered.[48]

Early cases were identified almost simultaneously in January 1981 in New York, San Francisco, and Los Angeles. The first case was a thirty-one-year-old male model who arrived at UCLA with a severe fungal infection. Diagnosing him was difficult, and he was treated as a victim of a rare infection. Soon, however, other unusual cases began turning up around the country, nearly all in homosexuals.[49] Finally, the common cause was uncovered and the deadly new disease identified.

The medical community was confronted with a frightening prospect: a gruesome disease for which there was no known cure and a group of recklessly promiscuous carriers. The disease was horrible enough when confined to the homosexual community, but equally disturbing were increasing reports of the transmission of AIDS to innocent parties: to heterosexual partners of bisexuals, to hospital patients receiving transfusions of AIDS-contaminated blood, to hemophiliacs dependent on regular infusions of new blood for life, to infants born to mothers with AIDS. As syndicated columnist Patrick Buchanan described it:

So long as AIDS appeared to be confined to active homosexuals, to a handful of Haitian refugees and to drug abusers using contaminated needles, there seemed no danger of a city-wide or national panic. It is now established, however, and becoming widely known, that AIDS can be transmitted through routine transfusion of blood donated by AIDS carriers. The evidence: the rising toll among the nation's small population of hemophiliacs, among whom AIDS has become the second most common cause of death.[50]

Homosexuals and drug abusers are the largest segment of society affected, yet "given the fact that the virus is transmitted through sexual contact, through the traces of blood and needles and other drug paraphernalia and from mother to newborn infant, one can envision many possible chains of infection, which leave no segment of the U.S. population completely unaffected by the threat of AIDS."[51] Indeed, the fastest growing group of reported AIDS patients in 1988 was not adults but children.[52]

Worrisome to health care workers is the possibility that one can be infected with AIDS if blood penetrates skin or mucous membranes, a fact which represents a "small but definite occupational risk for health-care workers."[53]

AIDS will continue to be with us for some time. Extrapolation studies by the Public Health Service estimate that 1.5 million people in the U.S. are infected with HIV, the virus that causes AIDS. The best current evidence is that each one infected will eventually come down with the disease. And, barring some cure, each of them will die of AIDS. While the increase in new cases has slowed as AIDS works its way through a homosexual population that is smaller than advertised, the loss of life has been substantial.

Regrettably, experts are seeing a second great wave of AIDS infections in the inner city, riding a crest of hard-core drug use and sexual promiscuity. In 1989, C. Everett Koop, former surgeon general, said:

> Everything that turns up confirms heterosexual spread, numerically and geographically.... Most recent estimates are that there will be, in the year 2000, a hundred million people who are HIV-positive.[54]

It is no wonder that AIDS has replaced cancer as the nation's most feared disease. Although there have been some concerns that AIDS might break out into the general population, the possibility of the breakout predicted by Dr. Koop is still a matter of some controversy among medical scholars.

A ten-year study of homosexual men in San Francisco finds that promiscuity is again on the rise. Among the findings presented by Robert Stempel of the San Francisco General Hospital to the Eighth International Conference on AIDS:

> The mean number of annual sex partners decreased from 80 before 1984 to 12 in 1988, but increased to 22 by 1991; the mean number of annual anal intercourse partners decreased from 36 in the early 1980s to 2 in 1989, but increased to 4 in 1991.[55]

7d. "Gay people, in fact, are less violent and less likely to commit child abuse."

Homosexual behavior has lead to extreme violence.

Approximately one out of ten homicides in San Francisco is the result of sadomasochistic sex among homosexuals.[56]

The homosexual movement is frequently blasé about violence.

As frightening as the statistics is the nonchalant way such violence is handled in the homosexual press. Typical is an *Equal Time* report of a rally on January 6, 1984, in the heart of a homosexual residential neighborhood in San Francisco. The report describes the rally without apparent disapproval. At the rally, some nine thousand people protested the release of Dan White, the San Francisco city council member who shot to death George Moscone, the mayor, and an openly homosexual city council member, Harvey Milk. White was found guilty only of voluntary manslaughter by a twelve-member jury. The keynote speaker at the rally was "Sister Boom-Boom," one of a group of drag-queen "nuns" called the Sisters of Perpetual Indulgence.

The "Sisters" appear around San Francisco dressed as nuns with a flagrantly homosexual flavor. The crowd, stirred to a frenzy by Sister Boom-Boom, heard him say that Councilman White's days were numbered: "Yesterday was the last day Dan White could spend knowing that he would live through the day. Today, Dan White begins a life sentence, and I'm sorry to say I don't think it's going to be a long one." As the speeches went on, men tossed black "Dan White Hit Squad" buttons over the crowd. Buttons were quickly grabbed and pinned on dozens of shirts and jackets. Thousands in the crowd sang along with a rendition of "Oh, Danny Boy," singing "Oh, Danny, where you gonna go? Someone's gonna find you, wherever you go."[57]

THE AIDS SPIN

Homosexual activists are a primary source of myths about AIDS.

Myths have been spread about AIDS. But the myth-spreaders have generally been homosexuals, trying to put a spin on what would seem a disease that clearly indicts homosexual practices. Even the establishment media have by now reported the story.

In "The AIDS Mythology: Misinformation Overstates Epidemic, Understates Funding for Research," Lou Kilzer identifies nearly every part of the AIDS spin promoted by homosexuals as a myth. He writes,

We all know the story:

AIDS is an exploding epidemic ravaging America. Once confined to gay men and a few other "high-risk" groups, it has now jumped into the population as a whole to threaten gay and straight, male and female, young and old alike.

The battle against AIDS is being fought by scientists who are severely under-funded but nevertheless have managed to make tremendous progress in understanding the disease. Special gratitude is due to the U.S. scientist who discovered the AIDS virus and to those who later determined how it kills immune system cells.

It's a story of universal tragedy and desperate hope. It is compelling. It is frightening.

And it is fiction. Every element is either a distortion or a lie....

The truth is that the rate of new infections has dropped dramatically, heterosexual transmission remains rare. AIDS now receives more federal research money than any disease except cancer. And despite a decade of investigation, science has not made much progress toward prevention or cure. In fact, there are indications that delays in certain research may have added to the death statistics.[1]

SPENDING

Kilzer goes on to say:

AIDS is often portrayed as the abandoned stepchild of U.S. biomedical research, strapped for funds and forever coming up short against other, less controversial diseases.

In fact, the opposite is true: AIDS is the darling when it comes to research dollars. On a per-patient basis AIDS spending outstrips every other major disease by far.

The federal government alone spent $53,745 on research and education for each AIDS death in the United States in 1990, more than 15 times the $3,241 spent per cancer death and 58 times the $922 per death spend on heart research.[2]

NUMBERS OF INFECTED

Kilzer continues:

In 1986, the CDC (Centers for Disease Control) estimated that 1 million to 1.5 million Americans were carriers of HIV....

Today, the CDC says 1 million Americans are infected—the low end of its 1986 estimate. Gone are predictions of 4 million to 9 million other cases.

The scaling back has been handled quietly in the government, and the media haven't been quick to correct their headlines....

OVERESTIMATING RISK TO THE POPULACE

Kilzer quotes one scientific observer as saying:

If someone from CDC tells me that there are a million people infected, I'll say, "Wait a second. It's 1992 and a half here; you told me there were a million people infected back in '88. [In 1986] they said 1.5 million."

Now I say: 'Which time were you lying?' What I'm saying is, if it's a million now, it was much less back then....[3]

Correcting bad numbers and false impressions can be difficult, in part for political reasons. AIDS activists have made the disease a civil rights issue and in numbers there is strength.

Whelan noted New York's experience three years ago when city officials scaled back their estimates of the HIV-infected population from 500,000 to 200,000. An immediate storm of protest exploded from many gays who feared their perceived political mass would shrink.[4]

It is clear from Kilzer's article that the CDC contributed to these myths. They widely overestimated the number of homosexuals in the population and were unwilling to admit what they had done. Instead of being forthright with what they had known for some time, CDC grew silent and decided to let the statistics catch up with the earlier estimates.

8b. "AIDS is not a gay disease. It is everyone's disease."

Homosexuals frequently overstate the heterosexual AIDS risk.

The bogus claim that AIDS is a disease of "all of us" is exposed in Michael Fumento's article, "Do You Believe in Magic?"[5] Fumento reviews various studies on the subject and documents an "ongoing war against reality."

The best evidence now is that heterosexuals have not been at substantial risk for contracting AIDS simply because they do not commit the sexual acts most closely linked with efficient AIDS transmission. While all agree AIDS has spread among heterosexuals, not all agree that the spread will be substantial. The Centers for Disease Control's chief epidemiologist, Dr. Harold Jaffe, has said: "Those who are suggesting that we are going to see an explosive spread of AIDS in the heterosexual population have to explain why this isn't happening."[6]

Even though a measure of controversy surrounds the future scope of the disease, one thing is not controversial. Homosexuals have been the principal recipients and transmitters of the AIDS virus—70 percent of all AIDS cases have occurred in homosexuals. In some states and in Europe, the percentages are even higher.[7]

Why are homosexuals the principal victims of AIDS? The answer is not complicated. With sexually transmitted AIDS, the overwhelming risk factor is anal intercourse, especially for the passive or recipient partner. According to B. Frank Polk, director of the Johns Hopkins University's component of the Multicenter AIDS Cohort Study, "In gay men, 95 percent or more of the infections occur from receptive anal intercourse."[8] And the American Journal of Public Health reported that in one study of 240 men who became infected with AIDS, all but four had engaged in anal sex as a receptor.[9]

An additional cause, of course, is the incredible level of homosexual promiscuity:

> Lately, thanks to AIDS, the word "promiscuity" has begun to acquire an unfavorable connotation among homosexuals, but not so long ago it was carried as a badge of honor, if not a defining condition of homosexuality itself. It is certainly a defining characteristic of AIDS sufferers.[10]

Even at the beginning of the developing crisis in 1985, sixty-nine percent of men having three or more sexual partners the previous month agreed with the statement, "It is hard to change my sexual behavior because being gay means doing what I want sexually."[11] So far, therefore, the principle purveyors and victims of AIDS have been homosexuals themselves.

Homosexual militants often seek to muzzle those who have sought to expose the truth about AIDS.

Those who have reported that the spill over of AIDS into the heterosexual population has been exaggerated have been brutalized, indeed censored, for their opinions. Consider the example of Michael Fumento himself when he revealed the systematic overstatement of the risks of heterosexual AIDS in a book called *The Myth of Heterosexual AIDS*. He details the censorship of his book in an article in *National Review* in December, 1993. When his book was reviewed in *Newsday* magazine, the reviewer was Jack Schwartz. Schwartz received a number of death threats, and seven to eight anonymous calls a night, merely for reviewing Fumento's book (Leslie Kaufman, "Beat the Press," in The Washington Monthly, Mar. 1993, p. 35) and for reporting that the public wrongly thought that AIDS was the number-one health threat at a time when it was number eleven. An Albany newspaper reporter was the subject of a barrage of abusive mail and intimidation. Harassment unheard of by groups opposing gay rights are standard by gay rights militants themselves.

8c. "The bias of the government is shown by its refusal to deal with AIDS and to commit the necessary resources to deal with it."

The disease of AIDS demonstrates how much political clout the gay rights activists wield.

The way our government has treated AIDS is an example of how much power homosexuals have, not how little:

a. It is the first disease in which the rights of transmitters have taken front stage over traditional public concerns, which focus on preventing transmission to the uninfected. Imagine, if you will, that this was more risky to heterosexuals, like syphilis. Did anyone in past syphilis epidemics seriously advance anti-discrimination measures to protect syphilitics? Were groups created to engender sympathy for PWSs (people with syphilis)? Did great waves of indignation pour down on Washington for not spending more dollars to defeat syphilis so Americans could continue to be sexually promiscuous without fear of infection? Did public health officials hide from health professionals, or public health reporting records, the syphilitic patient's identity?

b. Why should a society spend vast sums on a disease that is largely preventable by simple behavioral steps: avoiding sodomy, dirty-needle drug abuse, and carelessness in our blood banks? The massive sums spent on this disease seems counter-intuitive. Is it not more important to focus on the non-preventable diseases that claim far more victims: breast cancer; Alzheimer's; other cancers? The gay rights activists are really arguing that society owes it to those who commit sodomy to find a way at whatever public expense to let them continue to do it without risk of AIDS.

c. Why doesn't society treat sodomy like smoking and initiate a wide-scale effort to discourage people from engaging in it? This sanitized talk of exchange of body fluids is so vague. Why not tell people that anal sodomy is dangerous and should not be engaged in? Why not promote education programs that show clearly the dangers of the homosexual lifestyle?

d. The disproportionate amount spent on AIDS is staggering. AIDS research is funded at ten times the rate of cancer research if considered on a per death basis—over twenty times if considered on a per patient basis (Michael Fumento, "What You Can Do to Avoid AIDS," in the Washington Monthly, Dec. 1992, Vol. 24, No. 12, p. 46). In Britain, as described in F. LaGard Smith's excellent book, *Sodom's Second Coming,* the government there spends $75 for every person who dies of heart disease, $433,000 for every person who dies of AIDS.[12]

8d. "Until the government starts spending enough money to find a cure, the best we can do is AIDS education efforts in our schools, with a special emphasis on condom use."

Emphasis on condoms and removal of stigma on homosexual sodomy is counterproductive.

The now conventional wisdom in the United States is that homosexual behavior should be permitted in circumstances that allow education of the homosexuals to various risk factors. If homosexuals are forced underground, the rationale has it, there will be more and riskier sexual relations and thus more AIDS. That analysis is not only counter-intuitive but is not borne out anywhere in hard facts. One need only compare the spread of HIV infection in St. Petersburg, Russia, where homosexuality was illegal until 1992, and major American cities. As of June 1992, 4.2 million patients had been tested for HIV infection in St. Petersburg and .002 percent were found to be HIV positive, a rate 200 times lower than the infection rate here.[13]

One study revealed that condoms are only effective in preventing HIV infection about sixty-nine percent of the time. A study by Dr. Susan Weller of the University of Texas Medical School, suggested that the public at large may not understand the difference between "condoms may reduce risk of" and "condoms will prevent" HIV infection. She said it is a disservice to encourage the belief that condoms will prevent sexual transmission of HIV.[14] Dr. Weller concluded that "high-risk behaviors probably should not be avoided, but be eliminated; and condom usage considered a secondary strategy in prevention."[15]

CHAPTER 9

THE "PRIVACY" APPEAL:
Are Sexual Behaviors Entitled to Confidentiality?

9a. "What people do in their own bedrooms is nobody's business but theirs."

Society has an interest in regulating private behavior that is illegal or has social costs.

The past few decades have seen the rise of an idea peculiarly well suited to the individualism of modern America and to a prevailing obsession shared by several successive "me" generations. It is the idea that some crimes have no victims and therefore are not society's business. The law should keep its nose out of people's affairs, the theory goes, unless harm is being done to someone else.

This theory, a favorite of the American Civil Liberties Union, makes a neat distinction between crimes with victims—robberies, murders, arson, fraud—and crimes without victims—prostitution, pornography, drug use, consensual sodomy. It asks society to accept any behavior even if morally repugnant unless there is clear evidence of victimization of others. The old idea that there is a public morality that gives many significant, although intangible, social benefits is rejected, as is the Christian view that the morality of society is the most important determinant in its success and progress. "Righteousness exalteth a nation," wrote Solomon, "but sin is a reproach to any people" (Proverbs 14:34). Many who reject individualism in economic matters, however, rush to embrace it in moral matters, believing that tolerance demands a hands-off attitude.

Like all political misconceptions (at least those that attract adherents), there is a germ of truth to this analysis. A free society requires tolerance of diverse ideas. That government is indeed best that governs least. A free country leaves room for the free play of individual choices and decisions. But the idea of the victimless crime overlooks two key ingredients in human relationships: the centrality of morality and the power of influence.

As Jesus taught in the Sermon on the Mount through the metaphor of salt and light, the most important factor in human progress is the moral one. A virtuous people is a free and prosperous people, a proposition recognized by such diverse thinkers as Washington, Hamilton, Madison, and Jefferson. Economists such as Max Weber recognized the "Protestant work ethic" as a key factor in economic growth. Modern criminologists, such as Harvard's James Q. Wilson, recognize that moral training is the best antidote to crime. Historians such as Edward Gibbon agree on the principle cause of the collapse of the Roman Empire: moral rot. Good morals percolate through society and influence it toward good character, which in turn has an unmistakable impact on society at large. Bad morals work insidiously to cause decay. Christians believe that it is not the economic determinism of Marx, nor the sexual determinism of Freud, nor the evolutionary determinism of Darwin that best explains the meaning of history, but the moral determinism of the Bible. And that determinism spreads through society, not by some kind of decree, but by moral ideas.

Science recognizes the power of influence. A pebble dropped in the lake sends waves that lap to the farthest shore. Even more significant is the influence of complex interrelationships among men. "None of us liveth to himself," Paul says (Romans 14:7). The Bible teaches that all men have the same nature. We are all members of one organic whole. And our bond of physical relationship is strengthened by the universal interdependence of men upon one another. Men are dependent on other men for their education, their support, their nurturing, their protection, and their moral ideas.

The idea of victimless crimes is often simplistic.

The simplistic idea of the victimless crime ignores the tangible influence of public morality on society. The idea is rightfully suffering attrition in our times. More people are coming to realize that ideas have consequences. A good example is the current debate on pornography. Pornography has long been the primary example of the consensual victimless crime. What a person reads in the privacy of his bedroom, the ACLU briefs state, is nobody's business but his own. Others have begun to understand, whether or not they credit statements made by Ted Bundy about the role of pornography in his descent to barbarous behavior, how much such sordid material affects the society outside the bedroom. There is a spill-over effect of that material on others. In some cities, feminists have sought the passage of a law making the sale of pornography a violation of women's civil rights, because it demeans women.

Common sense suggests a broadening of the concept of the victim. A visitor to San Francisco, trying to walk his child through streets filled with pornography, prostitutes, and transvestites, can no longer believe that these ideas have no impact on others, despite their consensual nature. A visitor to a vice squad's portrait gallery of prostitutes, each shown successively after a sequence of arrests, reveals the horrible price paid by the prostitute.

The law itself has never adopted the concept of a victimless crime. Some libertarians rally around slogans that suggest the law has no place intruding into the privacy of a person's bedroom. Like most slogans, it is better chanted than analyzed. In fact, the law always has had a discrete interest in private bedrooms:

• *What goes on in the bedroom*: If what goes on in the bedroom has detrimental social consequences—incest, for example, or statutory rape—the state has a right to intervene, regardless of whether there was consent.

- *Who can use the bedroom with protection of marriage laws:* The state is unashamed to set rules on who can get married and who can get divorced.

- *The consequences of bedroom activity:* The law allows courts to inquire of acts inside bedrooms, after the fact, to determine the paternity of children, to enter private homes to determine custody and guardianship of children, and to set appropriate visitation rights conditional on fulfillment of requirements the court finds necessary.

- *The business bedroom:* The criminal courts are interested in what goes on in a brothel behind pulled curtains because it can affect individuals, community health, and families, and impose substantial social costs on society.

- *The number of wives in the bedroom:* Few societies are willing to sanction polygamy, no matter how private and consensual. While courts have recognized a legitimate zone of privacy, they have never accepted the simplistic appeal to leave unanalyzed private, consensual sexual activity. They know better.

For the same reason, the law cannot ignore the influence of sodomy. The existence of public homosexuality in our times has a powerful influence on the kind of society we have—the clothes we wear, the music we listen to, the preaching we hear from our pulpits, the treatment given our children, the lives lived by homosexuals themselves. We live, as philosopher Richard Weaver once said, in an increasingly effeminate culture. Homosexual author Dennis Altman has called the influence so great that it amounts to "the homosexualization of America."[1]

Homosexual influence is detrimental to society.

In analyzing whether homosexual conduct can be prohibited by ordinary statutes, therefore, it is important to consider whether homosexual influence in society is beneficial or detrimental. What is the influence of homosexuality?

Homosexuality's detrimental impact on society can no longer be disguised. Homosexual conduct injures others through spill-over effects, the homosexuals themselves, the latent homosexuals recruited into overt conduct, and society at large.

The medical dangers of homosexuality have already been discussed. The evidence can no longer be ignored. Homosexuals threaten communities with hepatitis, exotic infections, and AIDS. The new findings on AIDS have destroyed the gay rights' slogan that so long as homosexuals don't injure anyone, what they do is their business. If promiscuous homosexuals are capable of causing death through sexual contact, their slogan becomes irrelevant. Homosexual acts pose a medical threat not only to homosexuals, but also to those who need blood and to innocent partners of bisexuals. One homosexual said that, although he had AIDS, he never told his frequent sex partners because he was afraid of losing his sexual opportunities.[2] Is it reasonable to suggest that this is an isolated case? AIDS, which can be controlled through behavior change, also creates an enormous expense for the community. An assistant director of the San Francisco public health department claims the "average hospitalization of an AIDS patient runs four months and costs $80,000."[3] Homosexual acts are not "victimless crimes."

9b. "People have a constitutional right to do whatever they want to if it's consensual and doesn't affect some third party."

There is no right to homosexual sodomy based on a constitutional right to privacy.

On the privacy issue, Judge Robert Bork reports on how he learned from a famous colleague at the Yale Law School, Alex Bickel, that his uncritical acceptance of the privacy rationale was simplistic.

Suppose, he said, that on an offshore island there lived a man who raised puppies entirely for the pleasure of torturing them to death. The rest of us are not required to witness the torture, nor can we hear the screams of the animals. We just know what is taking place and we are appalled. Can it be that we have no right, constitutionally or morally, to enact legislation against such conduct and to enforce it against the sadist?[4]

In making such an argument, homosexuals rely on cases that interpret the Constitution as forbidding government interference with private decisions. And so, for example, a consensual "right of privacy" has been held to protect decisions about education and child-rearing, marriage, and more recently, contraception and abortion.[5] Homosexuals have argued from these cases that just as the law cannot unconditionally forbid a couple to use birth control, it cannot forbid two consenting adults to commit sodomy in the privacy of a bedroom.[6]

Although homosexuals had some initial success in state and federal courts using such arguments, the Supreme Court settled the question in Bowers v. Hardwick (1986).[7] Mr. Hardwick had brought suit in federal district court, challenging the constitutionality of the Georgia statute that criminalized consensual sodomy. He lost at the district court level, but won an appeal to the Court of Appeals, which held that the Georgia statute violated his fundamental rights. The Supreme Court disagreed. In a vigorously written opinion, Justice White pointed out that any fundamental liberties protected by a right to privacy must be "implicit in the concept of ordered liberty," or deeply rooted "in the nation's history and tradition." Because sodomy was traditionally a criminal offense in all states, to find that a right to engage in anal or oral sodomy was deeply rooted in this nation's history and tradition or is "implicit in the concept of ordered liberty" would be "at best facetious." Summing up, the Court said:

And if Respondent's submission is limited to the voluntary sexual conduct between consenting adults, it would be difficult, except by fiat, to limit the claimed right to homosexual conduct while leaving exposed to prosecution adultery, incest and other sexual crimes, even though they are committed in the home. We are unwilling to start down that road.[8]

In a concurring opinion, Justice Burger pointed out the moral dimension:

> To hold that the act of homosexual sodomy is somehow protected as a fundamental right would be to cast aside millennia of moral teaching.[9]

Justice Burger's opinion paralleled a recent circuit court decision from the District of Columbia Court of Appeals which had approved the discharge of a homosexual from the military. Finding homosexuality "a form of behavior never before protected and indeed traditionally condemned," that court held that its decision should be based on constitutional principle, not on shifting public opinion.[10] Such federal decisions have left homosexuals two options: convince state courts that there is a right to commit sodomy under the state constitution, or convince legislators to repeal the statute.

More recently, a three-judge panel tried to reverse clearly settled law by finding constitutional protection for a homosexual in the military. The case was of some instantaneous celebrity. But the celebrity was short-lived. The entire District of Columbia Federal Circuit was called into assembly *en banc* (not just the three judges, but all judges on the circuit court in the District of Columbia), and took the extraordinary step of reversing the decision decisively—rebuffing the Clinton administration, which wanted only a limited review. It held that there was no constitutional protection for homosexual sodomy.

Because homosexual activists have been unable to convince the courts that their sexually deviant behavior should be given special protection, they have tried to work harder on Congress, state legislatures, and city councils. The passage of gay rights laws would inevitably lead to the repeal of sodomy laws.

9c. "We want nothing more than to be left alone."

Homosexuals want prominence not privacy.

Notwithstanding the barbed thickets of common perceptions and common sense, homosexuals in the last decade have been making demands, sometimes quite successfully, on several fronts. These demands have one objective. As Dennis Altman writes in *The Homosexualization of America*, "The emergence of the modern gay movement [was] characterized by a willingness to demand not just tolerance but *total acceptance* and by a new militancy in making these demands" (emphasis added).

The strategic vision of "total acceptance" articulated by homosexuals such as Altman and others means public legitimacy, credibility, and community endorsement: in short, making sexual deviance as acceptable as sexual normality.

Homosexuals have a vision of the future far outside the mainstream of American life. Already the dim outlines of that future are being sketched by those on the cutting edge of homosexual ideology. Coming into view is the homosexual vision of a world where all sexual activity is placed beyond the rule of moral norms. The final destination for this ideology is a city of polymorphous and perverse sexuality where anything goes.

The final expression of this view will come in the push to legalize sex with children. It is already talked about by members of the homosexual community. It has long been an objective of many militant members of the homosexual movement. What appears shocking to us today may not be so shocking tomorrow.

CHAPTER 10

AIN'T NOBODY IN HERE BUT US CHICKENS:
How Homosexuals Seek To Put the Best Foot Forward, Even While Carrying Water for Child Molesters and Others

10a. "You distort homosexual behaviors by stereotypes. We are monogamous, too."

Homosexuals represent a broad spectrum of behaviors—all of which they seek to protect.

The movement tries to put its best foot forward. It does so by using carefully chosen spokesmen and seeding sympathetic stories to the media. It also tends to distort the true nature of homosexual behavior by claiming through its advocates that many homosexuals are monogamous (including the speaker making the claim), and that the movement should not be judged by its extremes. The trouble with this argument is manifold:

a.   One need not talk about extremes in the homosexual movement. One need only talk about medians. The median male homosexual has had upwards of five hundred male sex partners, making suspect the view that the spiritual and relational aspects of such "unions" dominate the merely physical. One should have the right to take into account that few heterosexual males have had such an obsessive fixation with anonymous sexual encounters that they have had five hundred female partners. Such behavior reveals something about the person, heterosexual or homosexual.

b.   Does the gay rights activist want the laws to be interpreted to protect only monogamous or nearly monogamous homosexuals, or does he want to include the 500- or 1,000-partner people? If the latter, why should we not talk about them in our debate? Does he believe the sadomasochist homosexual ought to be within the protection of the law? What about the man-boy lover? If he believes a homosexual ought to be protected in a state where same-sex sodomy is criminal, does he believe a man-boy lover ought to be protected where that activity is prohibited? If the law is to be widely applied, we need to know the characteristics of *all* the people it will protect, not just some of them.

c.   What does the speaker mean by "monogamous"? When I pressed one person I was debating about whether he was "actually" or "essentially" monogamous, he said, "Eighty, eighty-five times out of a hundred." I mentioned that was not a definition that would satisfy most wives: only fifteen sexual episodes outside of marriage in the last one hundred! For most homosexuals, monogamy means they have continuously lived with one partner for some time. It rarely means they have not supplemented their diet with other partners.

Homosexuality is, like all forms of behavior, a continuum. It reaches from casual thoughts and impulses to temptations, from temptations to discrete acts, from acts to habits, from habits to an entrenched lifestyle. Psychologists historically have called homosexuality "latent" or "overt." Not everyone with homosexual tendencies acts out his behavior, just as not everyone with temptations to steal, steals. Unless the inclination comes together with the opportunity, such latent tendencies may never crystallize into behavior. But the norm is promiscuity.

"Homoerotic art" gives insight into the homosexual lifestyle.

The norm also, unfortunately, is often bizarre. One need only survey "homoerotic art." In the Mapplethorpe exhibit, called "The Perfect Moment," the following was pictured:

[A] finger inserted into a penis; a man urinating into the

mouth of another man; two photos of children, a boy and a girl, with their genitals showing; and three photos showing anal penetration with a bull whip, a cylinder, and…a man's fist and arm.[1]

This is an insight into the homosexual lifestyle whose public image is far different.

10b. "The real child molesters are heterosexuals."

Homosexual pedophilia is defended by many homosexuals.

A popular book in homosexual bookstores is *Paedophilia: The Radical Case*, by Tom O'Carroll (Boston: Alyson, 1982). O'Carroll proudly notes, "I am a pedophile."[2] Among other things, O'Carroll complained that he was fired after having fallen in love with thirty-three boys, some as young as eleven. "They had not just taken away my livelihood. That was a trifling matter. The real crime was to stop me being of use, to myself or anyone else. To children, to individuals who needed me. To boys like Chris; I found myself hating the parents who had come between us."[3]

The furor over the introduction of books by a publisher of books on pedophilia into the New York City public school curriculum has been much discussed. Few people have actually read the text of such books as *Daddy's New Roommate* and *Heather Has Two Mommies*. Such books routinely seek to normalize these relationships. Indeed, occasionally to glorify them. In *Daddy's New Roommate*, for example, the following plot is described:

My Mommy and Daddy got a divorce last year.

Now there's somebody new at Daddy's house.

Daddy and his roommate Frank live together,

Work together,

Eat together,

Sleep together,

Shave together,

And sometimes even fight together.

But they always make up....

Mother says Daddy and Frank are gay.

At first I didn't know what that meant.

So she explained it.

Being gay is just one more kind of love.

And love is the best kind of happiness.

Daddy and his roommate are very happy together,

And I'm happy too![4]

The growing influence of pedophilia and its alarming dimensions have been noted in an FBI report,[5] which includes the following facts: One child sex ring in North Syracuse, New York, boasted over twenty thousand customers. A guide called "Where the Young Ones Are" listed 378 places in fifty-four cities in thirty-four states where a child could be found for sexual services. Seventy thousand copies of the guide were sold for five dollars each in just over thirteen months. Katherine Wilson, the "Kiddy Porn Queen" arrested in Los Angeles in 1982, had a mailing list of thirty thousand customers who sodomized children.

Child pornography sales exceed five hundred million dollars annually. Pedophilia is a growing subculture because of the lobbying effect of groups who argue for "children's sexual rights." This rationale, promoted by homosexual activists, was influential in reducing the "age of consent" to sixteen in Switzerland and twelve in Holland (unless parents object).[6] At the forefront of this battle are the homosexuals. And, like militant homosexuals generally, the homosexual pedophile is promiscuous. According to the director of the Sexual Behavior Clinic at the New York State Psychiatric Institution, the typical pedophile has molested sixty-eight children.[7]

But there are additional injuries inflicted on children beyond direct sexual abuse. A prime part of the gay rights agenda is societal blessing on same-sex marriages. Laws are being proposed around the country to permit marriage for homosexual couples. The existence of a gay rights ordinance might well be interpreted by a court to bar discrimination against homosexuals in the marriage relationship. Such an outcome, however, could have a serious and sexually disorienting effect on children.

How is a child to behave with two male or two female parents? How is he to respond to their relationship with each other and to their relationship with him? How is he to understand true femininity or true masculinity when his most significant role models are homosexual parents?

What about the child raised in a single-parent home by a homosexual? What happens to the child who is exposed to the homosexual's lover? Role models do have an impact. Common sense suggests that problems exist for the child who has never observed a normal parental relationship.

Many homosexuals are candid about their defense of child sex.

The amount of pedophilic behavior is easy to dismiss or underestimate. As one more candid homosexual has admitted:

> Nobody is fooled when we proclaim that the gay movement has nothing to do with kids and their sexuality.... Many of us—both women and men—had our first homosexual experience with partners who were older than ourselves.[8]

As attorney Eileen Scheff, a member of NAMBLA (North American Man/Boy Love Association), puts it,

> "[We must] empower our children to be able to make consensual decisions, and not to be coerced...to challenge the authority, to challenge the church, to challenge the priest, to

challenge the teacher, and have the right to have sex if they want to, and have the right not to have sex if they don't."⁹

The literature of pro-pedophilia propaganda is growing. Among other books published by Alyson Press, the publisher of *Daddy's Roommate*, are: *Macho Sluts* by Pat Califia; *Spartacus International Gay Guide; The Lesbian S/M Safety Manual; Gay Sex: A Manual for Men Who Love Men;* and *The Age Taboo,* which asserts that man/boy love is a civil rights issue and rejects "child molester" labeling.¹⁰ As Pat Califia says in *The Age Taboo:*

> Boy-lovers and the lesbians who have young lovers…are not child molesters. The child abusers are priests, teachers, thera-pists, cops and parents who force their stale morality onto the young people in their custody.¹¹

10c. "We're not asking for special protection for illegal activity of any kind."

The political power of the gay rights movement often influences peo-ple to turn a blind eye to pedophilia.

The growing threat of pedophilia caused enough concern to trig-ger an article by John Leo of *U.S. News & World Report.* He points out:

> Child molesters don't just hang around playgrounds. They apply for jobs at schools, camps, the Boy Scouts, Big Brothers, YMCAs. 'Boy lovers' love to work where the boys are.¹²

Leo points out that the press widely ignored the story of Peter Melzer, fifty-three, a teacher who was caught on video tape urging another public school employee to keep his membership in NAMBLA (North American Man/Boy Love Association) a secret until he had received tenure. Melzer teaches physics and science at the Bronx High

School of Science, one of the city's most prestigious schools. He is on the NAMBLA steering committee. As Leo points out, he has offered advice on enticing children into sex: "Leave a pornographic magazine someplace where he's sure to find it."[13]

Although the City Board of Education knew for years that Melzer was a man/boy lover, "nobody wanted to take responsibility for making a decision," as a special investigator for the school system later reported.[14] Melzer served as a delegate to the various international conferences on pedophilia among the "intellectually elite of child molesting."[15] The progress made by such man/boy lovers is frightening. NAMBLA is a member of the International Lesbian and Gay Association. The Association includes pedophiles in its call "to treat all sexual minorities with respect."[16] The group has marched in gay parades in New York and San Francisco on Gay Rights Day. Indeed, the editor of the Journal of Homosexuality, John DeCecco of San Francisco State University, is on the board of the Dutch pedophile journal, Piadika. As Leo points out:

> When I asked him why, he said, 'They needed a psychologist.' No. They 'need' respectability, and DeCecco is providing some. The culture is now so soft minded that many will listen to any self-styled victim group, perhaps even pedophiles. That's why it's crucial to keep them out of the schools.[17]

The North American Man/Boy Love Association (NAMBLA) is carrying the ideology of the homosexual movement to its natural conclusion. If there is no such thing as perversion and if sex is good, the exercise of the merely physical appetite, then why should children be denied this good?

NAMBLA takes the view that sex is good, that homosexuality is good not only for adults, but for young people as well. "We support all consensual sexual relationships regardless of age. As long as the relationship is mutually pleasurable and no one's rights are violated, sex should be no one else's business."[18]

Or as NAMBLA puts it again:

Sexual liberation cannot be achieved without the liberation of
children. This means many things. Children need to gain control over their lives, a control which they are denied on all
sides. They need to break the yoke of "protection" which
alienates them from themselves, a "protection" imposed on
them by adults—their family, the schools, the state, and prevailing sexual and social mores.[19]

So much for the ideology. The concrete proposals will surely follow. Again, NAMBLA has an idea:

There is no age at which a person becomes capable of consenting to sex. The age of sexual consent is just one of many
ways in which adults impose their system of control on children.... The state is the enemy of freedom, not its guarantor.
The best evidence against the argument that children cannot
consent to sex, including with adults, is the fact that millions
do it anyway.[20]

Two homosexuals reviewing my first book said in reply to my
concerns about pedophilia that man-boy lovers needed special protection because they were the most discriminated against people in the
homosexual community. They went on to say, "If Magnuson were not
a homophobic and erotophobic, he would see nothing wrong with sex
between an adult male and an eight-year-old boy." Such is the destiny
to which some homosexual militants want to push us.

CONCLUSION:
Informed Answers to Gay Rights Questions

Before you get on the plane, make sure you know the final destination.

The shocking tolerance shown by many segments of the homosexual movement toward sex with children is a fitting ending to our analysis. We must follow the train of argument to its final conclusion. Homosexual activists have shown skill in presenting their positions to a skeptical public: They are victims; their demands are limited; they ask for elemental fairness.

But underlying their ideology is a troubling set of assertions that serve as premises for continuing expansions of their claims to social acceptance. They believe there are no ultimate norms for sexual expression. To suggest guard rails—boundaries—for the sex drive is to them mere moralizing. They argue that all sex is normal sex, at least if it is consensual; the appetite for sex, expressed through an interest in same-sex partners or peculiar forms of sexual behavior, is as natural and diverse as the appetite for food.

We have demonstrated the weakness of those premises. But the propaganda mill of moral relativism continues to pound away at public consciousness. And once these premises are accepted by society at large, once the carefully constructed guard rails disappear, there is no stopping the plunge down the precipice.

If sex is a good and healthy recreation without norms, why deny it to children? Why be concerned about incest? Why not seek to promote and encourage sexual experimentation of all kinds in our schools' sex education classes? Why not welcome adoption by man-boy lovers? Why discourage pornography? Why make prostitution illegal? What ultimately is special or particularly valuable about the traditional family?

If there is no real right and wrong in sex, why should there be any rules at all?

This is why some public spokesmen for homosexual rights can piously distance themselves from pedophilia, even while their rationale inevitably leads to NAMBLA's—the North American Man/Boy Love Association's—conclusions. The man-boy lovers are simply more consistent in working out the ultimate consequences of the gay rights arguments.

He who says A must therefore say B, the logician tell us. Follow the argument to its ultimate conclusion. When we do so, we see that what is at stake is not some modest inclusion in an obscure municipal human rights ordinance but children, the family, and civilization itself. Dennis Prager put it well:

> ...It is very easy to forget what Judaism has wrought and that Christians have created in the West. But those who loathe this civilization never forget. The radical Stanford University faculty and students who chanted "Hey, hey, ho, ho, Western civ has got to go," were referring to much more than their university's syllabus.

> And no one is chanting that song more forcefully than those who believe and advocate that sexual behavior doesn't play a role in building or eroding a civilization.[1]

ENDNOTES

Introduction: *Why This Book Is Important*

1. Thomas Sowell, *Inside American Education: The Decline, the Deception, the Dogmas*, (New York, NY: The Free Press, A division of Macmillan, Inc., 1993).

2. "TR Rates the Professors: The Excellent, the Mediocre, and the Atrocious," *Texas Review,* September 1987, p. 7.

3. *The Public Interest,* No. 112, Summer 1993, pp. 60-83.

4. Ibid., Dennis Prager p. 82.

5. Thomas Sowell, *Inside American Education,* (New York, NY: The Free Press, A division of Macmillan, Inc., 1993).

6. "History of the Earth," *The Confidential Guide: Courses at Harvard Radcliffe 1987-88,* (Cambridge, MA: The Harvard Crimson Inc., 1987), p. 63.

7. "The Best and the Bogus," *Northwestern Review,* (November 17, 1989), p. 5.

8. "What Am I in For?" *California Review of Berkeley,* (November 1989), p. 9.

Chapter 1

The Agenda: *What Homosexuals Really Want*

1. Dennis Altman, "The Movement and Its Enemies," in *The Homosexualization of America* (Boston, MA: Beacon Press, 1982), pp. 112-13.

2. Carl B. Harding, "Letter," in *Mattachine Review,* (August 1956), pp. 35-36.

3. Dennis Altman, *Homosexualization of America,* p. 113.

4. Ibid.

5. See Anthony Cassano, "Coming Out in the Churches," *Pastoral Renewal,* (March 1981), pp. 71-72.

6. Ibid.

7. Some statutes authorizing dismissal of teachers for "immorality" have been found unconstitutionally vague. For example, see *Burton* v. *Cascade School District Union High School,* 353 F. Supp. 254, D. Ore., (1973).

8. Homosexual behavior is not, of course, generally protected. Title VII of the Civil Rights Act of 1964 has been held, for example, not to protect homosexuals. See *DeSantis* v. *Pacific Tel. and Tel.,* 13 CCH EPD par. 11,335, D. Cal., (1976).

9. Some states, for example, have allowed homosexuals to adopt their partner. Other courts differ. Some courts have not permitted those who simulate sexual roles to marry (*Baker* v. *Nelson,* 291 Minn. 310, 191 N.W.2d 185 [1971]) and, on occasion, have denied custody to homosexual parents (*Chaffin* v. *Frye,* 45 Cal. App. 3 39, 119 Cal. Rptr. 22 [1975]).

10. See Duluth Human Rights Ordinance, Chapter 29C, Duluth City Code E, (1959 as amended).

11. George Orwell, "Politics and the English Language," in *Shooting An Elephant ,* (Harcourt Brace & Co., 1950).

12. F. L. Smith, *Sodom's Second Coming: What You Need to Know About the Deadly Homosexual Assualt,* (Eugene, OR: Harvest House Publishers, 1993), p. 235.

13. 1972 Gay Rights Platform, drawn up at the National Coalition of Gay Organizations convention, (Chicago,IL: 1972) Enrique Rueda, *Homosexual Network,* pp. 202-3.

14. "Gays in the Classroom," *New York Post,* (11 July 1979).

15. Gay Teachers Association, "A Bill of Rights for Gay Teachers and Students" (Albany, 1982).

16. O'Leary and Vida, "Lesbians and the Schools," paper circulated at the Nebraska International Women's Year Conference, Lincoln, (25-26 June 1979).

17. This is a partial listing of the 62 platform demands found in "The Official 1993 March on Washington for Lesbian, Gay and Bisexual Rights and Liberation Program Guide," published by the Committee for the March on Washington, Inc.

18. Enrique Rueda, *Homosexual Network*, p. 129. It is often a short step from equality to "preference."

19. "Universities in the Queer 90s," *Campus* (Winter, 1994), p. 18.

20. Ibid.

21. See "Same Sex Marriage and the Constitution," *Legal Problems and Family Law* (University of California, Davis, CA: *Law Review* 6 [1973]): p. 275.

22. Mary Beth Murphy, *Milwaukee Sentinal* , "Bisexual Pastor Chose to Wed, Saved Ministry", (Milwaukee, WI: April 23, 1993).

23. Mike Royko, "Gays in the Military?" *Chicago Tribune,* (January 14, 1993).

24. "Sexual Fixation," *Campus* (Winter, 1994), p. 13.

Chapter 2

The Approach: *Take the Offensive, and Stay Away from the Behavior*

1. F. L. Smith, *Sodom's Second Coming: What You Need to Know About the Deadly Homosexual Assault,* (Eugene, OR: Harvest House Publishers, 1993), p. 21.

2. The colloquy took place in an Advocates Debate on WCCO TV on the Sunday before the vote on the St. Paul gay rights ordinance, (April 23, 1978).

3. Chief Justice Stone apparently coined the phrase, saying that "prejudice against discrete and insular minorities may be a special condition, which tends seriously to curtail the operation of those political

processes ordinarily relied upon to protect minorities, and which may call for correspondingly more searching judicial inquiry." United States v. Carolene Prods, 304 U.S. 144, 152 N. 4 (1938).

4. Dennis Prager, "Homosexuality, the Bible, and Us," *The Public Interest*, No. 112, (Summer 1993), p. 76.

5. F. L. Smith, *Sodom's Second Coming*, (Eugene, OR: Harvest House Publishers, 1993), p. 26.

6. Ibid., p. 81.

7. See K. Jay and A. Young, *The Gay Report* (New York, N.Y.: Summit Books, 1979), p. 253 ff.

8. Charles Laurence, "Playboy chief admits to being bisexual," in the *London Daily Telegraph*, (Mar. 13, 1993), p. 1.

9. Dennis Prager, "Homosexuality, the Bible, and Us," *The Public Interest*, No. 112, (Summer 1993), p. 74—citing David E. Greenberg, *The Construction of Homosexuality*, (Chicago,IL: University of Chicago Press, 1988).

10. Angela Phillips and Jill Rakusen, *The New Our Bodies Ourselves* (London: Penguin, 1989), pp. 193, 209, 213.

11. Charlotte Bunch, *Lesbians and the Women's Movement*, (1975)—as quoted in Dennis Prager, "Homosexuality, the Bible, and Us," *The Public Interest*, No. 112, (Summer 1993), p. 74.

12. Jill Johnson, *Lesbian Nation: The Feminist Solution* (1973)—as quoted in Dennis Prager, "Homosexuality, the Bible, and Us," *The Public Interest*, No. 112, (Summer 1993), p. 74.

13. "Menacing Gays Could Be Made a Crime," *Seattle Post-Intelligencer*, (11 May 1984).

14. Quoted by Edwin J. Haeberle in "Swastika, Pink Triangle and Yellow Star: The Destruction of Sexology and the Persecution of Homosexuals in Nazi Germany," *Hidden From History: Reclaiming the Gay and Lesbian Past*, M. Duberman, et al (NY: NAL Books, 1989).

15. Samuel Igra, *Germany's National Vice,* (London: Quality Press, Ltd., 1945).

16. Ibid.—As quoted in *Family Research Report,* Family Research Institute, (Sept.-Oct. 1992), p. 1.

Chapter 3

The Authentication: *Why It Is Important for Homosexuals to Misrepresent Who and How Many They are (and Were)*

1. Testimony of Bryant Welch, Executive Director for Professional Practice, APA, before American Bar Association, (Feb. 6, 1989).

2. J.M. Sundet, et al, "Prevalence of risk-prone sexual behavior in the general population of Norway," *Global Impact of AIDS,* (Liss: 1988), pp. 53-60—as quoted in *Family Research Report,* Family Research Institute, (May-June 1992), p. 1.

3. M. Melbye and R.J. Biggar, *Amer J Epidemiology* 1992, pp. 135, 593-602—as quoted in *Family Research Report,* Family Research Institute, (May-June 1992), p. 1.

4. G.M. Breakwel and C. Fifc-Schaw, "Sexual Activities and Preferences in a United Kingdom Sample of 16- to 20-Year-Olds," *Archives Sexual Behavior,* (1992), pp. 21, 271-293—as quoted in *Family Research Report,* Family Research Institute, (May-June 1992), p. 1.

5. S. Roberts and C. Turner, "Male-Male Sexual Contact in the USA: Findings From Five Sample Surveys, 1970-1990," *J Sex Research,* (1991), pp. 28, 491-519—as quoted in *Family Research Report,* Family Research Institute, (May-June 1992), p. 5.

6. G. Remafedi, et al, "Demography of Sexual Orientation in Adolescents," *Pediatrics,* (1992), pp. 89, 714-721—as quoted in *Family Research Report,* Family Research Institute, (May-June 1992), p. 5.

7. *Family Research Report,* Family Research Institute, (Nov.-Dec. 1992).

8. Murray Edelman, Director of Voter Research and Surveys (VRS), as cited in *Lambda Report,* No. 1, (Feb. 1993), p. 3.

9 Dr. J. Gordon Muir, "Homosexuals and the 10% Fallacy," *The Wall Street Journal,* (March 31, 1993).

10. Ibid.

11. Lynette Burrows, "Sunday comment," in *The Sunday Telegraph,* p. 20.

12. Patrick Rogers, "How Many Gays Are There?" in *Newsweek,* (Feb. 15, 1993), Society, p. 46.

13. Ibid.

14. "All Things Considered," National Public Radio, (Apr. 15, 1993), findings published in *Journal for Family Planning Perspectives,* Dr. John Billy and Albert Klassen.

15 F. L. Smith, *Sodom's Second Coming,* (Eugene, OR: Harvest House Publishers, 1993), pp. 47-8.

16 Dennis Prager, "Homosexuality, the Bible, and Us, *The Public Interest,* No. 112, (Summer 1993), p. 65—citing David E. Greenberg, *The Construction of Homosexuality* (Chicago, IL: University of Chicago Press, 1988).

17. Ibid.

18. Ibid., p. 64—citing David E. Greenberg, *The Construction of Homosexuality* (Chicago: University of Chicago, 1988).

19. Dr. R. E. Allen, Professor of Classics, Northwestern University, *New York Times,* (2/27/93).

20. Dennis Prager, "Homosexuality, the Bible, and Us," p. 70.

21. Classicist Eva Keuls, as quoted in Prager, p. 70.

22. See, for example, *Family Research Report,* (July-August 1993), p. 6.

23. *Report on Teen Suicide*, Department of Health and Human Services (August 1989).

24. See William Dannemeyer, *Shadow in the Land*, (Ignatius, 1989), pp. 211, 214 for a discussion of AIDS reporting.

25. Enrique Rueda, *The Homosexual Network*, (Greenwich, Conn.: Devin-Adair Publishers, 1982), p. 129.

26. Ibid., p. 129.

27. See discussion in William Dannemeyer, *Shadow in the Land*, p. 89 ff, (Ignatius, 1989); and F. L. Smith, *Sodom's Second Coming*, (Eugene, OR: Harvest House Publishers 1993), pp. 148-149.

28. Ibid., p. 243.

29. David Briggs, Associated Press, (10/20/93).

30. As discussed in F. L. Smith, *Sodom's Second Coming*, (Eugene, OR: Harvest House Publishers, 1993), pp. 148-9.

31. See Bullough, "Challenges to Societal Attitudes toward Homosexuality in the Late 19th and Early 20th Centuries," *Social Science Quarterly* 58 (June 1977), p. 37.

32. See Ivan Illich, "Disabling Professions" in *Disabling Professions*, Ivan Illich, et al. (London: Marion Boyers Publishers, 1977).

33. Garret, et al., *Homosexuality in the Western Christian Tradition* (London: Longmans, Green and Co. 1955), p. 73.

34. Ibid.

35. Enrique Rueda, *Homosexual Network*, p. 246.

36. Ibid., p. 248.

37. *America*, (25 June 1977), p. 558.

38. "Homosexuals in Religious Life," *The Tablet*, (26 December 1981), p. 19.

39. Enrique Rueda, *Homosexual Network*, chapters 6 and 7.

40. Irving Bieber, et al., *Homosexuality: A Psychoanalytic Study of Male Homosexuals,* (New York, N.Y.: Basic Books, 1962), 18.

41. For an excellent and balanced discussion of the intersection of the gay rights movement and American psychiatry, see R. Bayer, *Homosexuality and American Psychiatry,* (New York: Basic Books, 1981), p. 102ff.

42. R. Bayer, *Homosexuality and American Psychiatry* (New York, N.Y.: Basic Books, 1981), p. 103.

43. Ibid.

44. Ibid., p.105.

45. Karl Menninger, *Introduction to the Wolfenden Report,* (New York: Stein & Day, 1963), p. 7.

46. Bayer, *Homosexuality,* p. 140.

47. Ibid., p. 141.

48. Ibid., p. 140.

49. Ibid., p. 141.

50. Ibid., p. 167.

51. Ibid., p. 102—as cited by Congressman William Dannemeyer, *Shadow in the Land: Homosexuality in America* (San Francisco: Ignatius Press, 1989), pp. 25-26.

52. Personal conversation with the author.

53. Socarides, "Homosexuality," p. 120.

54. Ibid., p. 119.

55. N. Meredith, "The Gay Dilemma," *Psychology Today*, (January 1984), p. 56.

56. S. Hadden, "Homosexuality: Its Questioned Classification," *Psychiatric Annals*, (April 1976), p. 46.

57. Dr. Charles Socarides, "Homosexuality," p. 119.

58. Ibid., p. 123.

Chapter 4

The "All God's Children" Claim: *Why Homosexuals Claim That Nature Makes Them Do It (Sometimes), Even Though the Assertion Is Demonstrably False*

1. Wainwright Churchill, *Homosexual Behavior among Males* (New York, N.Y.: 1967), 101—as quoted in Congressman William Dannemeyer, *Shadow in the Land: Homosexuality in America* (San Francisco, CA: Ignatius Press, 1989), p. 47.

2. Robert Frumkin, *The Encyclopedia of Sexual Behavior* (New York: 1967), p. 439—as quoted in Congressman William Dannemeyer, *Shadow in the Land,* (San Francisco, CA: Ignatius Press, 1989), p. 47.

3. H.C. Resnik and Marvin Wolfgang, *Sexual Behaviors: Social, Clinical, and Legal Aspects* (Boston, MA: 1972), p. 397—as quoted in Congressman William Dannemeyer, *Shadow in the Land,* (San Francisco, CA: Ignatius Press, 1989), p. 47.

4. William H. Masters, Virginia E. Brown, and Robert C. Kolodny, *Human Sexuality,* (Boston, MA: 1984), pp. 319-20—as quoted in Congressman William Dannemeyer, *Shadow in the Land,* (San Francisco, CA: Ignatius Press, 1989), p. 48.

5. Dr. Charles Socarides, "Homosexuality," p. 118. See also T. Hoult, "Human Sexuality in Biological Perspective: Theoretical and Methodological Considerations," *Journal of Homosexuality,* 9 (Winter 1983), pp. 137-55.

6. Dr. Albert Ellis, *Homosexuality: Its Cause and Cure*, (New Yorkm N.Y.: 1965)—as presented in *Shadow in the Land* by Congressman William Dannemeyer, (San Francisco, CA: Ignatius Press) pp. 50, 55.

7. Edmund Burglar, *Homosexuality: Disease or Way of Life,* (New York, N.Y.: 1962) pp. 281-82—as presented in *Shadow in the Land* by Congressman William Dannemeyer, (San Francisco, CA: Ignatius Press) pp. 50, 56.

8. As quoted in *The Family Research Report,* Family Research Institute, (Mar.-Apr. 1993), p. 1.

9. Dr. Charles Socarides, "Homosexuality," pp. 137-55.

10. Dr. James McCary, *Sexual Myths and Fallacies,* (New York, N.Y.: Van Nostrand Reinhold, 1971), p. 94.

11. Joe Dallas, "Born Gay?" in *Christianity Today,* (June 22, 1992), p. 22.

12. Darrell Yates Rist, "Are Homosexuals Born That Way?" in *The Nation,* (Oct. 19, 1992), Vol. 255, No. 12, p. 424.

13. Dr. Charles Socarides, "Homosexuality," pp. 123-24.

14. Enrique Rueda and Michael Schwartz, *Gays, AIDS and You,* p. 72.

15. Ibid.

16. Dr. Charles Socarides, "Homosexuality," p. 124.

17. Many people trying to escape from homosexuality could benefit from the help of a support group. The secular group Homosexuals Anonymous has chapters across the nation. Exodus International is an educational organization that gives referrals to Christian support groups around the world (P. O. Box 2121, San Rafael, CA 94912, 415-454-1017).

18. Joseph Nicolosi, as quoted in F. L. Smith's *Sodom's Second Coming,* (Eugene, OR: Harvest House Publishers, 1993) p. 83.

19. Anthony Falzarano, "Good News: Gays Can Change," *Lambda Report,* No. 1, (Feb. 1993), p. 8.

20. Roy Cohn is the famous New York "super lawyer" who initially made his mark as counsel to Senator Joe McCarthy in the televised McCarthy hearings, and later represented the rich and famous in many high-profile legal battles.

21. Dennis Prager, "Homosexuality, the Bible, and Us," *The Public Interest,* No. 112, (Summer 1993), pp. 73-74—citing Letita Anne Peplau, "What Homosexuals Want," *Psychology Today,* (March 1981).

22. Dennis Prager, "Homosexuality, the Bible, and Us," p. 73.

23. Tom Lehrer once called the U.S. Army the ultimate equal opportunity employer because it "did not discriminate on the grounds of race, creed, color...or ability."

24. "Neither present-day endocrinological tests nor microscopic or clinical examinations have revealed any physiological differences between a heterosexual and a homosexual." Dr. James McCary, *Sexual Myths and Fallacies* (New York: Van Nostrand Reinhold, 1971), p. 94.

25. Dr. Charles Socarides, "Homosexuality," p. 118. See also Irving Bieber, *Homosexuality: A Psychoanalytic Study of the Male Homosexual* (New York, N.Y.: Basic Books, 1962).

Chapter 5

The Argument: *How Doing Sexually Deviant Acts Can Make a Minority Worthy of Civil Rights Protection*

1. *Poe* v. *Ullman* 367 U.S. 492, 522, n.3 (1961), J. Harlan dissenting.

2. *Gay Law Students Association* v. *Pacific Telephone and Telegraph*, 24 Cal.3d 458, 488, 595 p2d, *592, 610, 156* Cal.Rptr. 14, 32 (1979).

3. See E. Boggan, M. Haft, C. Lister, J. Rupp, and T. Stoddard, *An ACLU Handbook: The Rights of Gay People*, rev. ed. (1983), p. 17.

4. States that have criminal sodomy laws are Alabama, Arizona, Arkansas, Florida, Georgia, Idaho, Kansas, Kentucky, Louisiana, Maryland, Massachusetts, Michigan, Minnesota, Mississippi, Missouri, Montana, Nevada, New York, North Carolina, Oklahoma, Pennsylvania, Rhode Island, South Carolina, Tennessee, Texas, Utah, and Virginia, and also the District of Columbia. Although most state sodomy statutes do not distinguish between homosexuals and heterosexuals, six states bar only homosexual acts of sodomy: Arkansas, Kansas, Kentucky, Missouri, Montana, and Nevada.

5. 478 U.S. 186 (1986). The Court said, "Precedent aside, however, Respondent would have us announce as the Court of Appeals did, a

fundamental right to engage in homosexual sodomy. This we are quite unwilling to do."

6. The law of privacy has not provided much solace for homosexuals. As one proponent of gay rights puts it, "The courts have refused, on non-existent grounds, to extend this right [of privacy] to homosexuals" (J. Baer, *Equality Under the Constitution* [Ithaca, N.Y.: Cornell University Press, 1983]), p. 231. Courts have held, for example, that the right of privacy does not protect extramarital relationships. J. S. Mill's classic statement on privacy held that society shall not meddle with "purely personal conduct."

7. The Ninth Circuit has recently held that discrimination against homosexuals in the military violates the equal protection clause. The decision conflicts with other decisions and is unlikely to be followed by the Supreme Court. The Supreme Court has granted unequivocal suspect status to only three classes: race, national origin, and alienage. See *State* v. *Walsh* 713 SW.2d 508, 510 (MO. 1986).

8. Various forms of disparate treatment of homosexuals have been permitted by the courts in employment situations. Flaunting a homosexual lifestyle has been held, for example, to justify government termination of employment. See *Singer* v. *United States Civil Service Commission*, 530 F.2d 247, 9th Cir., (1976).

9. As cited in *Lambda Report*, No. 1, (Feb. 1993), p. 7.

10. Chief Justice Stone apparently coined the phrase, saying that "prejudice against discrete and insular minorities may be a special condition, which tends seriously to curtail the operation of those political processes ordinarily relied upon to protect minorities, and which may call for correspondingly more searching judicial inquiry." *United States* v. *Carolene Prods*, 304 U.S. 144, 152 N. 4 (1938).

11. "Developments in the Law: Sexual Orientation and the Law," *Harvard Law Review* 102 (1989), pp. 1508, 1668, n. 51.

12. Commentators in favor of gay rights generally ignore, or pass by lightly, the substantial evidence that homosexual behavior has damaging consequences, including enormous physical dangers, both to homosex-

uals and to public health. (See previous chapter.)

13. For a pro-gay rights approach to sexual orientation law see Rivera, "Queer Law: Sexual Orientation Law in the Mid-80s," *University of Dayton Law Review* 11 (1986), p. 275; Chatin and Lefcourt, "Is Gay Suspect?" *Lincoln Law Review* 8 (1973), p. 24; Dressler, "Judicial Homophobia: Gay Rights Biggest Roadblock," *Civil Liberties Review,* (Jan.-Feb. 1979), pp 19, 22. See also Revere, "Our Strait-laced Judges: The Legal Position of Homosexual Persons in the United States," *Hastings Law Journal* 30, (1979), p. 799.

14. *Bowers* v. *Hardwick,* 478 U.S. 186, 106 S.Ct. pp. 2841, 2847 (1986). See also Romans 1:24-27; 1 Corinthians 6:9-11; Jude 7.

15. F. L. Smith, *Sodom's Second Coming,* (Eugene, OR: Harvest House Publishers, 1993).

16. Usdansky, "Gay Couples, by the Numbers," *USA Today,* (April 12, 1993), pp. 1A, 8A.

17. Enrique Rueda, *The Homosexual Network,* (Greenwich, Conn.: Devin-Adair Publishers, 1982).

18. H. Brown, *Familiar Faces, Hidden Lives: The Story of Homosexual Men in America Today* (Orlando, Fla.: Harcourt Brace Jovanovich, 1976).

19. Coleman, "Washington Gay Vote," *Washington Post,* (21 April 1979).

20. S. Steele, "Business Affairs," *The Voice,* (27 March 1981), p. 30; see generally Dennis Altman, *The Homosexualization of America,* (Boston, MA: Beacon Press, 1982), p. 18ff.

21. Enrique Rueda, *Homosexual Network,* p. 177.

22. Dennis Altman, *Homosexualization of America,* p. 33.

23. G. Becker, *The Economics of Discrimination,* (Chicago: University of Chicago Press, 1963).

24. Bob Dart, "Activists See This Decade as the Gay 90's," Cox News Service, (February 1993)—as quoted in F. L. Smith's *Sodom's Second Coming,* (Eugene, OR: Harvest House Publishers, 1993) pp. 25-6.

25. Minnesota Committee for Gay and Lesbian Rights, *Working for the Equal Rights of Lesbians and Gay Men* (pamphlet).

26. Dr. Charles Socarides, "Homosexuality: Basic Concepts and Psychodynamics," *International Journal of Psychiatry* 10, (1972), p. 120.

27. William Dannemeyer, *Shadow in the Land,* (San Francisco, CA: Ignatius Press, 1989).

28. D.C. Code Ann. §§ 1-250 to 2557 (1981).

29. *Gay Rights Coalition of Georgetown University Law Center* v. *Georgetown University,* 536 A.2d 1 D.C. (1987). The court did hold that the university did not have to recognize or "endorse" the homosexual group.

30. Such laws always provide serious civil penalties (see, for example, the Minneapolis Human Rights Ordinance, Minneapolis City Code, as amended). Some ordinances make it a criminal violation, holding out ninety days in jail as a possible penalty.

31. The only exception to the general right of landlords to rent to anyone they please is embodied in civil rights laws that protect unchangeable characteristics based on biology (sex, race), historical accident (national origin), or belief system (religion). None of these narrowly defined exceptions protects immoral behavior.

32. "Men and Boys: The Boston Conference," *Gaysweek*, (12 February 1979), p. 9.

33. Psalm 1:1; Proverbs 2:16, 7:6-23, 9:6-7, 11:15, 20:4; Micah 2:2; Romans 1:28.

Chapter 6

The Amoral Orthodoxy: *How Homosexuals Promote the View That Sex Has No Moral Boundaries*

1. Dennis Prager, "Homosexuality, the Bible, and Us," *The Public Interest,* No. 112, (Summer 1993), p. 72.

2. Enrique Rueda, *Homosexual Network,* p. 246

3. Enrique Rueda, *Homosexual Network,* p. 246.

4. *Resources for Ministry,* Committee on Ministry to/with Gay and Lesbian Persons of the Minnesota Synod-Lutheran Church of America (undated).

5. "Statement on Homosexuality," Social Justice Committee, Minnesota Council of Churches (1982).

6. Ralph Blair, *An Evangelical Look at Homosexuality,* (Homosexual Community Counseling Center, 1972). Blair's views, of course, are his own, and do not reflect the opinion of the National Association of Evangelicals.

7. Lewis Smedes, *Sex for Christians,* (Grand Rapids, MI: Wm. B. Eerdmans Publishing Co., 1976), p. 73.

8. J. Rinzema, *The Sexual Revolution,* (Grand Rapids: Wm. B. Eerdmans Publishing Co., 1974).

9. Dennis Prager, "Homosexuality, the Bible, and Us," p. 68.

10. For this and the other tenets of the revisionist view listed below, see generally C. Philpot, *The Gay Theology,* (Plainfield, NJ.: Logos, 1977); J. Rinzema, *The Sexual Revolution.*

11. 2 Corinthians 5:17. See 1 Corinthians 6:11 for an application of this truth to the homosexual condition.

12. 2 Corinthians 5:16-21.

Chapter 7

The Avoidance Factor: *What Homosexuals Must Cover Up About Typical Same-Sex Lifestyles*

1. See, for example, J. Katz, *Gay American History* (New York: Thomas Crowell, 1976); M. Friedman and M. Rubin, *American Educator* 67 (1978), which claims, among others, Michelangelo and Alexander the Great. Homosexuals are on good ground when they claim Oscar Wilde or Walt Whitman, but stretch to include others on

little evidence. They claim, for example, the ancient Greek writers for their admiration of the beauty of young boys without pointing out that sexual contact with them was a capital offense in ancient Athens. A good example of overreaching the evidence is the case of Michelango. He is widely accused of homosexuality based on two things: his bachelorhood and allegations brought against him by Aretino, a notorious blackmailer. As Irving Stone, author of *The Agony and the Ecstacy*, a famous biography of Michelangelo, points out, "We did not find a scintilla of evidence to support the allegation that Michelangelo was a homosexual." Letter from Irving Stone to Abigail Van Buren, *Washington Star*, (20 April 1981).

2. Paul Walker, quoted in N. Meredith, "The Gay Dilemma," *Psychology Today*, (January 1984), p. 60. This is also a common theme in homosexual publications such as *The Advocate*, *GLC Voice*, and *Equal Time,* (the first a nationwide magazine, the last two Minneapolis-St. Paul area tabloid newspapers).

3. See generally, Michael Fumento, "Do You Believe in Magic?" *American Spectator Magazine,* (February 1992); "The AIDS Mythology," *Star Tribune Newspaper,* (Minneapolis,MN: July 5, 1992), p. 10A.

4. The health risks of homosexuality are nowhere more clearly seen than in the AIDS epidemic. See "The AIDS Epidemic," *Newsweek*, (18 April 1983), pp. 74-79; Glenn Wood and John Dietrich, *The AIDS Epidemic,* (Portland, OR.: Multnomah Press, 1990).

5. See Zygmund Dobbs, *Keynes at Harvard*, (New York, N.Y.: Veritas Press, 1963); A. Calder Marshall, *The Sage of Sex* , (New York, N.Y.: Putnam, 1959); H. Ellis, *Studies in the Psychology of Sex* , (New York, N.Y.: Random House, 1942).

6. To give one some idea of the perversity of these practices, they include eating, drinking, and being showered with the waste products of a partner ("water sports" and "golden showers"), inserting fists, forearms, bullwhips, or even gerbils into the rectum (resulting in a thoroughly modern medical procedure called the gerbilectomy) and, as

Mapple Thorbe's "homoerotic art" depicts, forcing fingers or other objects up the male member itself.

7. See F. DuMas, *Gay Is Not Good*, (Nashville, TN: Thomas Nelson Publishers, 1979).

8. K. Jay and A. Young, *The Gay Report*, (New York, N.Y.: Summit, 1979), p. 567.

9. Ibid., pp. 553-96, pp. 490-93.

10. Stephen Green, *The Sexual Dead-End*, (Broadview Books, 1992).

11. K. Jay and A. Young, *The Gay Report*, p. 500.

12. Ibid. p. 501; see also *Gayellow Pages*.

13. Dr. Charles Socarides, "Homosexuality: Basic Concepts and Psychodynamics," *International Journal of Psychiatry* 10 (March 1972), p. 119. For other psychiatric references, see I. Bieber et al., *Homosexuality*, (New York, N.Y.: Basic Books, 1962); H. Gershman, "Psychopathology of Compulsive Homosexuality," *American Journal of Psychoanalysis* 17 (1957), pp. 58-77; Edward Glover, *The Roots of Crime: Selected Papers on Psychoanalysis*, vol. 2 (London: Imago Publishing Co., 1960); S. Hadden, "What Outcome Can Be Expected in Psychotherapy of Homosexuals," *Medical Aspects of Human Sexuality* 5, (December 1971), pp. 96-100; M. Mahler, "On Human Symbiosis and Vicissitudes of Individuation," *Journal of the American Psychoanalytic Association* 15, (1967), pp. 740-63.

14. Enrique Rueda, *The Homosexual Network*, (Greenwich, CN.: Devon-Adair Publishers, 1982), p. 37.

15. Study, U.S. Centers for Disease Control (Atlanta, GA: 1982), reported in N. Meredith, "The Gay Dilemma," p. 56. See also A. Bell and M. Weinberg, *Homosexualities* (New York: Simon & Shuster, 1978), pp. 85-86.

16. K. Jay and A. Young, *Gay Report*, p. 250.

17. See Meredith, "Gay Dilemma," p. 58.

18. Enriquie Rueda, *The Homosexual Network*, (Greenwich, Conn.: Devin-Adair Publishers, 1982), p 57.

19. Ibid., p. 58.

20. See figures in Enrique Rueda, *Homosexual Network*, pp. 181-85.

21. Interview in C. Philpot, *The Gay Theology* (Plainfield, N.J.: Logos, 1977), p. 23.

22. The evidence is clear from such movements as the North American Man/Boy Love Association and the support of homosexual groups for elimination of laws governing minimum ages of consent for sexual acts. See also DuMas, *Gay Is Not Good*, pp. 105-6.

23. See Zygmund Dobbs, *Keynes at Harvard*; A. Calder Marshall, *Sage of Sex;* H. Ellis, *Studies in the Psychology of Sex.*

24. "Bill of Rights," Gay Teachers Association, (July 1977).

25. "Homosexual Love Away from School Is OK, Gay Teachers Say," *New York Post*, (11 July 1979).

26. Enrique Rueda, *Homosexual Network*, p. 73.

27. K. Jay and A. Young, *Gay Report*, pp. 275, 279, 281.

28. *Gay Community News*, quoting a speech by Virginia Apuzzo, executive director of the National Gay Rights Task Force, to two hundred educators at Harvard, (23 April 1983).

29. "Child Molesters Picketed," *Twin Cities Christian*, (5 July 1984).

30. Enrique Rueda, *Homosexual Network*, p. 175.

31. The removal was affirmed unanimously by the Minnesota Supreme Court. *State Board* v. *Winton*, NW 2d (MN: 1984).

32. *GLC Voice* Classifieds, (18 July 1984), p. 13.

33. See Enrique Rueda, *Homosexual Network*. See generally P. Buchanan and J. Muir, "Gay Times and Diseases," *The American Spectator*, (August 1984), pp. 15-18.

34. Enrique Rueda, *Homosexual Network*, pp. 52-53. See also T. Quinn, "The Polymicrobial Origin of Intestinal Infections in Homosexual Men," *New England Journal of Medicine* 309 (1983), pp. 576-82; David Ostrow et al., eds., *Sexually Transmitted Diseases in Homosexual Men* (New York, N.Y.: Plenum Medical Book Co.,

1982); L. Corey and K. Holmes, "Sexual Transmission of Hepatitis A in Homosexual Men," *New England Journal of Medicine* 302 (1980), pp. 435-38; Gerald Mandell et al., eds., *Principles and Practice of Infectious Diseases*, 3rd ed. (New York, N.Y.: John Wiley and Sons, 1990), pp. 2280-84, and references therein.

35. Katie Leishman, "AIDS and Syphilis," *The Atlantic Monthly*, (January 1988), pp. 20, 21.

36. Ibid.

37 E. Rowe, *Homosexual Politics* (CLA, 1984), p. 17.

38. P. Buchanan and J. Muir, "Gay Times and Diseases," pp. 17, 18. The remarkable incidence of hepatitis in homosexual men is noted throughout medical literature. See Corey and Holmes, "Hepatitis A in Homosexual Men"; Gerald Mandell et al., *Principles and Practice of Infectious Diseases*, pp. 2280-84 and references therein.

39. J. Kassler, *Gay Mens' Health* (New York, N.Y.: Harper and Row, 1983), p. 38.

40. David Ostrow et al., *Diseases in Homosexual Men*, p. 204.

41. See P. Buchanan and J. Muir, "Gay Times," p. 18.

42. See generally, *San Jose Mercury News*, (24 April 1980); "Sharp Increase in Hepatitis and Dysentery in San Francisco," *San Francisco Chronicle Examiner*, (23 April 1979); see also "The Advocate Guide to Gay Health" (1983); Gerald Mandell et al., *Principles and Practice of Infectious Diseases*, pp. 2280-84 and references therein.

43. David Ostrow et al., *Diseases in Homosexual Men*, pp. 204.

44. David Ostrow et al., *Diseases in Homosexual Men*, p. 204.

45. R. Henig, "AIDS: A New Disease's Deadly Odyssey," *New York Times Magazine*, (6 February 1983).

46. David Ostrow et al., "Hemorrhoids, Anal Fissure, and Condylomata Acuminata," *Diseases in Homosexual Men*, pp. 141-49.

47. G. Manligit et al., "Chronic Immune Stimulation by Sperm Alloantigens," *Journal of the American Medical Association* 251

(1984), pp. 237-41. See also J. Richards et al., "Rectal Insemination Modifies Immune Responses in Rabbits," *Science* 224 (1984), pp. 390-92; G. Shearer and A. Rabson, "Semen and AIDS," *Nature* 308 (1984), p. 230.

48. "The AIDS Epidemic," *Newsweek*, (18 April 1983), p. 74. See also G. Ahronheim, "The Transmission of AIDS," *Nature* 313 (1985):, p. 534; R. T. Ravenholt, "Role of Hepatitis B Virus in Acquired Immunodeficiency Syndrome," *Lancet* (1983), pp. 885-86; W. Winkelstein et al., "Potential for Transmission of AIDS-Associated Retrovirus from Bisexual Men in San Francisco to Their Female Sexual Contacts," *Journal of the American Medical Association* 255 (1986), p. 901; H. Jaffe et al., "National Case-Control Study of Kaposis Sarcoma and *Pneumocystis Carinii* Pneumonia in Homosexual Men," *Annals Internal Medicine* 99 (1983), pp. 145-57; Gerald Mandell et al., *Principles and Practice of Infectious Diseases*, pp. 2280-84 and references therein.

49. Ibid.—Other groups affected include intravenous drug users, hemophiliacs, and, more recently, heterosexual partners of bisexuals.

50. Patrick Buchanan, "AIDS, Homosexuals and Political Dynamite," *Washington Times*, (1 June 1983), p. 2C.

51. W. Heyward and J. Curran, "The Epidemiology of AIDS in the U.S." *Scientific American*, (October 1988), p. 78. The entire issue is devoted to "what science knows about AIDS."

52. Ibid. W. Heyward and Curran also report that transfusion of a single unit of HIV-contaminated blood is "very likely to result in infection", p. 79.

53. Ibid.

54. P. Dean, "America's New Family Doctor," *Minneapolis Star Tribune*, (24 November 1989), p. 29A.

55. *Lambda Report,* No. 1, (Feb. 1993), p. 3.

56. "Coroner Battles Sado-masochistic Injuries," *Associated Press*, (12 March 1981). See also *Blade*, (11 September 1981).

57. *Equal Time*, (25 January 1984), p. 3.

Chapter 8
The Aids Spin

1. Lou Kilzer, "The AIDS Mythology: Misinformation Overstates Epidemic, Understates Funding for Research," *Minneapolis Star Tribune,* (7/5/92), p. 1A.

2. Ibid., p.10A.

3. Ibid., p. 11A.

4. Ibid.

5. *The American Spectator,* (February 1992), pp. 16-21.

6. Michael Fumento, "AIDS: Are Heterosexuals at Risk?" *Commentary* 84 (November 1987), p. 22.

7. See W. Heyward and J. Curran, "Epidemiology of AIDS," p. 78.

8. Michael Fumento, "AIDS," pp. 22-23.

9. Ibid., p. 23.

10. Ibid.

11. L. McKusick et al., "AIDS and Sexual Behavior Reported by Gay Men in San Francisco" *American Journal of Public Health* 75 (1985), pp. 493-96.

12. F. L. Smith, *Sodom's Second Coming,* (Eugene, OR: Harvest House Publishers, 1993), p. 228.

13. A. O. Kozlov et al., "Epidemiology of HIV Infection in St. Petersburg, Russia," *Acquired Immune Deficiency Syndromes*, (1993), pp. 6, 208-212.

14. "A meta-analysis of condom effectiveness in reducing sexually transmitted HIV" *Social Science & Medicine, (*1993), pp. 36, 1635-1644.

15. Ibid.

Chapter 9

The "Privacy" Appeal: *Are Sexual Behaviors Entitled to Confidentiality?*

1. Dennis Altman, *The Homosexualization of America* (Boston: Beacon Press, 1982).

2. R. Henig, "AIDS: A New Disease's Deadly Odyssey," *New York Times Magazine*, (6 February 1983), pp. 28-44.

3. Norris, *There's Nothing Gay about Homosexuality,* (pamphlet available through Good Neighbors, Box 73, Clovis, CA 93612).

4. Robert H. Bork, *The Tempting of America,* (New York: The Free Press, 1990), p. 124.

5. *Griswold* v. *Connecticut* 381 U.S. 479 (1965), and *Roe* v. *Wade* 410 U.S. 1113 (1979).

6. See *Oklahoma City School Board* v. *National Gay Rights Task Force* 727 F.2d 1270 10th Cir., 1984; U.S., (1985).

7. *Bowers* v. *Hardwick,* 478 U.S. 186 (1986).

8. Ibid.

9. Ibid.

10. The Supreme Court appeared to follow the reasoning of an earlier decision in the District of Columbia Court of Appeals, *Dronenburg* v. *Zech*, in which Judge Bork upheld the discharge of a U.S. Navy petty officer who had repeatedly engaged in sodomy with one of his recruits. See *Dronenburg* v. *Zech* 741 F.2d 1288 (D.C. Cir., 1984).

Chapter 10

Ain't Nobody in Here but Us Chickens: *How Homosexuals Seek to Put the Best Foot Forward, Even While Carrying Water for Child Molesters and Others*

1. F. L. Smith, *Sodom's Second Coming,* (Eugene, OR: Harvest House Publishers, 1993), p. 110.

2. Tom O'Carroll, *Paedophilia: The Radical Case* (Boston,Ma Alyson 1982), p. 9.

3. Ibid., p. 28.

4. Michael Willhoite, *Daddy's Roommate* (Boston: Alyson Publications, 1991).

5. "Law Enforcement Bulletin," Federal Bureau of Investigation, (January 1984).

6. See *Washington Blade,* (9/6/91) and *Stonewall Union Reports,* (2/91).

7. Ibid.

8. Pat Califia in Daniel Tsang, ed., *The Age Taboo: Gay Male Sexuality, Power and Consent* (Boston and London: Alyson Publications/Gay Men's Press, 1981), p. 144.

9. *Family Research Report,* Family Research Institute, Nov./Dec. 1992.

10. See *Lambda Report,* No. 1, (Feb. 1993), p. 2.

11. Pat Califia, "Man/Boy Love and the Lesbian/Gay Movement," *The Age Taboo: Gay Male Sexuality, Power and Consent* (Boston and London: Alyson Publications/Gay Men's Press, 1981), p. 144—as cited in *Lambda Report,* No. 1, (Feb. 1993), p. 3.

12. "Pedophiles in the Schools," *U.S. News & World Report,* (10/11/93), p. 37.

13. Ibid.

14. Ibid.

15. Ibid.

16. Ibid.

17. Ibid.

18. Enrique Rueda and Michael Schwartz, *Gays, Aids and You* (Greenwich, Conn.: Devin-Adair Publishers, 1987), p. 67.

19. Ibid.

20. Enrique Rueda and Michael Schwartz, Gays, Aids and You (Greenwich, Conn.: Devin—Adair Publishers, 1978), p. 67.

Conclusion

1. Dennis Prager, "Homosexuality, the Bible and Us," *The Public Interest* No. 112, (Summer 1993), p. 82.